# Knees Lifted High
## *and*
## Toes Pointed

# Knees Lifted High
## *and*
# Toes Pointed

Marching to Sounds of Human Decency

DAVID DALKE
*Foreword by Taylor Clark*

RESOURCE *Publications* · Eugene, Oregon

KNEES LIFTED HIGH AND TOES POINTED
Marching to Sounds of Human Decency

Copyright © 2022 David Dalke. All rights reserved. Except for brief quotations in critical publications or reviews, no part of this book may be reproduced in any manner without prior written permission from the publisher. Write: Permissions, Wipf and Stock Publishers, 199 W. 8th Ave., Suite 3, Eugene, OR 97401.

Resource Publications
An Imprint of Wipf and Stock Publishers
199 W. 8th Ave., Suite 3
Eugene, OR 97401

www.wipfandstock.com

PAPERBACK ISBN: 978-1-6667-3008-1
HARDCOVER ISBN: 978-1-6667-2114-0
EBOOK ISBN: 978-1-6667-2115-7

JANUARY 26, 2022 8:22 AM

This story is dedicated to the students of the St. John, Kansas High School Marching and Concert Band 1934–1941

# Contents

*Foreword by Taylor Clark* | ix
*Inspiration for This Book* | xi
*Acknowledgments* | xiii
*Introduction* | xv

| | | |
|---|---|---|
| Chapter 1 | Passion and Decency | 1 |
| Chapter 2 | Positivity and Decency | 9 |
| Chapter 3 | Patience and Decency | 15 |
| Chapter 4 | Humility and Decency | 19 |
| Chapter 5 | Adversity and Decency | 23 |
| Chapter 6 | Trust and Decency | 29 |
| Chapter 7 | Making Room and Decency | 35 |
| Chapter 8 | Humor and Decency | 40 |
| Chapter 9 | Flexibility and Decency | 45 |
| Chapter 10 | Praise and Decency | 51 |

| Chapter 11 | Ethics and Decency \| 55 |
| Chapter 12 | Leadership and Decency \| 64 |
| Chapter 13 | Continual Fine-Tuning and Decency \| 70 |
| Chapter 14 | More Than Melody and Decency \| 74 |
| Chapter 15 | Shared Healing and Decency \| 79 |

Epilogue \| 90

# Foreword

Taylor Clark
Seventh Generation Stafford County Kansan
Future Music Educator

Born and raised I am a St. John, Kansas girl. It is my favorite place in the world, and I can't imagine having grown up anywhere else. I am so thankful for the lessons I learned and the people who helped raise me in this community. The only thing I love more than this community, is the St. John band. Music has always played a vital role in my life, so much so that I have decided to make it my career. When given the opportunity to meet with David Dalke about his father starting the St. John High School Band, I jumped on the opportunity. I was fascinated to learn more about the man who made the band a reality in my hometown. Mr. Dalke's love and passion for music resounded in pages of newspaper articles, stories, and photos. I am thankful to have learned more about the man who, in a way, is a part of why I want to be a band teacher, too. I hope to share my passion and love for music with my students just as Mr. Dalke did, and create something that is truly special in the community that I choose to serve. After all, music is the bridge that connects community.

# Inspiration for This Book

I sat in the newspaper office of the editor, settling in for an interview regarding my most recent book. Pictures on the walls and piles of old and current newspapers graced her crowded room, leaving no doubt as to her profession. We talked about how stories inspire people to examine what is important in their lives, especially in books and certainly on the pages of newspapers.

"That's what we do here," she said. "We tell stories. Now, let's talk about your next book. Why have you waited so long to write it? Why now?"

The question challenged me. I had asked it of myself for many years, having tucked the story of my dad's high school marching band inside my heart and soul. "Greatest years of my life," he used to say, as he would reminisce about being the Professor of Music in St. John, Kansas from 1934 to 1941. There was a story that had to be told, but why now? Why had I waited this long?

Twenty-two years ago I spent three days and nights in another newspaper office reading every article about the band from those miraculous years. I found a courtship and a marriage between a man named Jake and a little town on the mid-American high plains. I talked to twelve band members in their seventies who were part of that miracle. As they relived those days, they beamed with nostalgic enthusiasm. Their passion was contagious. I had to tell the story. So I wrote a little book called *Jake's Band*.

## Inspiration for This Book

I made copies of the book and sent it to all our grown kids and grandkids. No one else read the story except a local band instructor. Oh, and I actually researched how to write a movie script and developed the story into a hoped-for screenplay. I tested my writing with the actress Shirley Knight, who was born in the little Mennonite community of Goessel, Kansas, where my dad was born. She liked the story, tweaked it a bit, and encouraged me to keep pursuing my fledgling scriptwriting. It sits in a file drawer, untouched.

"Why now?" I finally had the answer. All my previous writings about those early years spoke of victorious results in competitions—but I had missed the essence of the story. There were poignant reasons why one hundred band members, morning after morning, regardless of weather, practiced their marching on streets so wide that eighteen-wheelers could rumble into town side by side. I missed why a group of people enthusiastically anticipated band concerts on those warm Saturday nights in the familiar town square, as farmers and families would greet one another and discuss the week's happenings. The cake was tasty, but what made it so? There was an answer. It was deeper than music.

Jake set out on a seven-year journey. He knew what it would take to develop a championship marching and concert band. It would be an exploration into the character of each young musician, previously unaware of their calling to "make music". He must model and inspire decency—the sounds of footsteps and harmonies would follow. With the support of his family, the school administration, and a struggling, depressed community, the story began. I tell it to you now.

# Acknowledgments

It is with a grateful heart I acknowledge the many people in my life who have supported the writing of this book. My spouse, Sheryl, has been there for me with constant compassion and understanding of my need to broadcast this story. Her continual reading of the manuscript and astute suggestions have been so lovingly offered. My grown children and eight grandchildren have spent many years hearing about the beauty of their grandpa's band. My friends have encouraged me to tell the musical miracle that occurred in a small town during those depressive years. A special thank you to each and every one of them.

My research has led me to the powerful historical influences that grace the pages of this book. My dad, Jake, created the story. He was one of seven siblings, having grown up in Goessel, Kansas, a sparsely-populated Mennonite community. He was a gifted athlete, musician, and he was a risk-taker with extreme creativity. Tucked deep inside his values was his belief in decency along with a practiced spirituality. My mom was his constant companion, who found meaning in her own musical pursuits as a music educator. She did not lose perspective as to the importance of balancing profession and parenting. She told my sister and me, after several moves we made as a family in our formative years, "I think the reason you and Judy seem so well-adjusted is because your dad and I never left your sides." I also thank my sister Judy for standing with me in this family history, both when we were younger and in our later years.

ACKNOWLEDGMENTS

One cannot write a story like *Knees Lifted High and Toes Pointed* without acknowledging the town—St. John, Kansas. The town was born in the early part of 1879, named after the Kansas Governor, John Pierce St. John. Three years later it was granted a charter to be the permanent county seat and became an oasis for travelers. People needed a place to settle and survive. In 1910 there were 791 residents, and when dad arrived in 1934 the population was 1500. The years were not kind to St. John, with continual dust storms and crop failures, but the townsfolk did not give up. The community welcomed the beginnings of a high school band and reveled in its success. I regret deeply that I cannot offer this story to each band member who put St. John on the map. Those students unequivocally trusted dad's leadership and vision. If they are still living, they are nearing 100 years old. Hopefully some of their family members will get a glimpse of the miracle. Of course, an integral part of the band's success came from each student's parents, the band mother's club, and the six members of the school board who hired Jake Dalke as their Professor of Music. I wish I could give a book to each of them personally. My spirit reaches out.

In the present moment my deepest gratitude is for my new friend, Larry Haise. Without him, this book would be searching for a measure of quality. His guidance has been invaluable to me.

# Introduction

*From 0 to 100 in seven years*

THE SCHOOL BOARD MEMBERS SAT QUIETLY.
Jake replied.
"Before I say yes to your kind offer, let me ask one last question. How many students do you have in your band?"
There was an embarrassing silence. Don Kitch, the superintendent of schools sheepishly replied:

> Well, Jake, we don't have a band. Oh, one of our young ladies plays her Grandpa's saxophone, but that's it. Now you know why we want to hire you—to develop a band. We need someone like you to lift our spirits. Our town is dying. The depression has hit us hard. Stores and banks are closing. Poverty is all around us. Crops are failing from all the dust storms. War is looming. Jake, we have very little to count on—maybe a sermon or two on Sundays gives us a temporary boost. We want to laugh and hope that life is worth living. We believe—no, we seriously believe—that maybe, just maybe, music might be the medicine we need. Are you up for the challenge?

The year was 1934.
In seven unbelievable years Jake created a band from 0 to 100 band members. Under his tutelage students learned to play their chosen instruments and to march with knees lifted high and

toes pointed at state fairs, small town parades and halftime performances during high school football games.

By 1941 the band put St. John, Kansas, and its 1,500 residents on the map by winning state, district, and three national concert and marching band contests in Omaha, Nebraska, Colorado Springs, Colorado, and Kansas City, Missouri.

The town had been reborn. Music was not only in the air but also in the hearts of a dispirited community. Amidst the hours and days of unexpected turmoil came the pounding of student footsteps marching up and down brick streets learning to walk in precisely straight lines. The early morning hours brought the blaring of John Phillip Sousa marches that pulled townsfolk to the curbs, coffee cups in hand, to hear the sounds of hope. Music had not resolved everyone's helpless feelings, but rather had embraced them—with hope.

Yes . . . 0 to 100 in seven years. How could this happen?

The answer is found in the now-brittle pages of a scrapbook Jake put together from the time he became the Professor of Music in this small western Kansas town until he left in 1941. As I explored the articles, pictures, and headlines, pieces of the yellowish worn pages fell to the carpet, looking like leaves shedding their beauty in the autumn. The story is all there. It is a course of events, some of them actual, and some as I imagined them to be. It is a seven-year odyssey of relationships. It is about a man who believed that life does not need to be mired down in the pain of hopelessness, but could be uplifted by music based on decency, bringing out the best in people.

Their beautiful sounds reverberated then. They echo today.

# CHAPTER 1

# Passion

*(strong, joyful motivation)*

# and Decency

"You need to stay on the farm. Your brothers and sisters need you to help with all the chores and harvesting. I need you to carry your share of the load. You have graduated from high school, and that is enough education. Jake, you must stay here and help us."

The year was 1928. With a college degree in music education, Jake set out to fulfill his dream, living out his passion to be a secondary education music instructor. As long as he could remember he wanted to teach young people how to play instruments and learn the beauty of sound, harmonies, and crescendos, and to march with knees lifted high and toes pointed. It was not an easy decision to leave the farm. Amid feelings of abandoning his family, he heard these words from his loving and compassionate mother,

"Jake, go and do what you must do. We will be all right."

His musical journey led him to teach briefly in two grade schools and one high school. Then he threw caution to the wind and applied for the position of "Professor of Music" in St. John. He accepted the position with courage and enthusiasm even though at times he thought about his father's penetrating words,

"Jake, we need you on the farm. This is where you belong."

There are times when passion overrules common sense. Jake made a faithful decision to accept the challenge of trying to pull this depressed and anxious community together with the sound of music. His family had taught him the virtues of tenacity in overcoming life's obstacles. Tilling the earth, season after season, taught him to cultivate his own life with trust and hope in rain and sunshine. He felt up for the task. His passion was driving him.

Alternatively chugging and gliding, his car made sounds that caused him to wonder if he would ever arrive at this little dot on the map. What would this town look like? Surely it would have more stores than his birthplace of Goessel, which had one long main street with a volunteer fire department, a co-op and a telephone office, where operators surreptitiously listened to juicy town gossip. As he turned off the main highway, he spotted the silver water tower reaching towards the sky like an overgrown lantern.

The bold print said **St. John**.

He had carefully disguised his clandestine journey from his family and most of his teaching colleagues. Like an adventurer not sure of what he would find, he began by exploring.

The town square was framed with large cement blocks intermittently spaced to separate the busy street from the soft grass. On the east side were Junior's Bakery and Rollie Benford's Barbershop. Howard Drug Store, the Post Office, Frank Sutton's Law Office and the local Bank were on the south. The west side of the square was not quite as busy with just Hattie's Dress Shop and Butch's Hardware Mercantile, and to the north sat Henning's Car Dealership plus a Five and Dime Store. The movie theater was a half block off of the square, as was the courthouse.

Jake, continuing to make one right turn after another, noticed signs of the times in the various store windows: "Support our Football Team," "Methodist Church Bazaar tonight," "Peaches – only 19 cents a can," "Ovaltine – large can 65 cents," "Palmolive Soap – 5 cents a bar," and, oh yes, "Don't Miss Will Rogers's New Movie – only 40 cents."

A few blocks from the downtown square was a scattering of churches, none Mennonite. *The Methodist Church looks rather inviting,* Jake thought. *If I take this job in the school, maybe I'll go there.*

South of town was the railroad station, where a few cars were parked waiting for the next train. He pulled up next to a family with three small children, all eagerly looking out their windows for the approaching Atchison, Topeka and the Santa Fe. Little did he know his future years would be spent in this very spot, loading and unloading his students for their contest travels.

He stopped by the news office to buy the eight-page daily paper.

"You new here?" asked the editor.

"Yes, I just drove in. I'm considering moving here."

"Well, take a newspaper. Put your money in your pocket."

Articles on each page of the paper were full of gloom. It was no secret. People everywhere were reeling from the most devastating years in American history. St. John was no different.

Only a few years prior the stock market had crashed, wiping out whole fortunes. Banks failed without warning, leaving the masses penniless. Thousands of folks were unemployed and dreadfully undernourished.

Besides the Depression, there were continual fears of another world war at the hands of the Germans and Japanese. The townsfolk were emotionally depleted. What was left? The square—yes, the town square.

**The setting for future band concerts**

On Saturday evenings everyone would spiffy up and gather to shop or just visit with one another. It seemed that the only hopeful thing in sight was the local high school football team with a possible triumph to celebrate from the night before, or maybe a victory this coming Friday.

This was the town Jake found.

"Are you Jake Dalke?" The amiable voice echoed down the hallway.

"Yes I am, you must be . . ."

"I'm Don Kitch, the superintendent and high school principal. Welcome. We sure appreciate your willingness to interview with us. We have heard many complimentary things about you, from your college days to your present teaching position in Ford. Everyone is really high on you."

"Well . . . that's awfully kind of you. I couldn't pass up the opportunity to meet you and the school board members. St. John is a little bigger than Ford, so I thought it might be a good move for me. Of course . . . if you all think so."

"Jake, let's go meet the board members. They are waiting for you right down the hall. Nervous?"

"A little. This is the first position I've applied for. The school board at Ford pursued me while I was at Bethel College, so this is the first time I've . . . "

"Listen, I need to warn you that not all of the board members believe we need a Professor of Music here in St. John. A couple of them are pretty content with our football program even though we haven't had the best of seasons lately. Just thought I should clue you in."

Jake followed Don into a small room with six men crammed in around an oblong table. Walter, Elmer, Harold, Butch, Henry and George stood and politely greeted him in an atmosphere laden with obvious curiosity. Don opened the meeting.

"Gentlemen, as you are aware, we are interviewing candidates for a new music position here in the high school. We've talked to three other interested parties, and today we have with us Jake Dalke, who has also applied for the position of Professor of Music. He comes highly recommended to us, and he's here to answer any questions you might have of him. You can refresh your memories by looking over his resumé he sent us, and then discuss how he might establish a music program in our high school."

Butch is the first to speak. He leans forward on his crusty elbows, makes direct eye contact and speaks with a determined voice.

"Jake, do you have any idea what you are getting yourself into if you accept this job?"

Jake responds, "I know these are tough times. I'm guessing this town needs some hope . . . something to look forward to. Maybe, just maybe, music can be an answer. If that is what you want, and we can work out the terms, then . . . well, I'm willing to give it a try."

Harold chimes in. "Are you saying music can lift the spirits of this town? We have a football team that handles that task. Now, we haven't been so red-hot lately, but we're looking forward to a mighty fine team, if not this year, maybe next year. Our coach is alright, but he can't keep losing forever. In fact, this town won't stand for it. We have some big, husky boys who are just itching to hit somebody. Truth is, Jake, music might be nice, but it will only fill in the gaps for those students who don't play sports, especially the girls."

Walter believes the board has enough information.

"I suggest we vote and get out of here."

Harold ignores him. He has more to ask Jake.

"You said something about your mother and brothers and sisters, but tell me more about your dad. As talented as you are, he must have encouraged all of you kids to play music. Sounds like a great man to me."

Jake looks down at the table contemplatively. Slowly he raises his head, leans forward and responds in a soft and serious voice.

"My dad is a hard worker, and as you know, it's not easy farming these days. He had a dream that all of us kids would stay on the farm and help him. Everyone stayed except me." Clearing his throat, he sits back in his chair, looking down once again.

Elmer is listening intently and speaks with sincere empathy.

"I think you know we have read your resumé and have checked your credentials with the principal at Ford High School, plus talked to several of the teachers. They all recommend you highly for this position. Truth is they hope we won't hire you so they can keep you directing their band. They believe you are the best left-handed director around these parts. Any questions you wish to ask of us?"

The interview continued. Jake asks many questions about the St. John community, the potential interest in forming a band, what churches were there, and lastly, what the salary would be. Money wasn't all that important to him. He had grown up to believe life's deepest meanings were found inside oneself, and that material possessions would come to those who were faithful to their beliefs and not greedy. Jake did have one last question for the six board members.

"How many students do you have in your band now?"

Don feels slightly chagrined in responding to the question.

"We don't have a band. There is only one girl in this school who plays an instrument. It's her grandad's saxophone. We have no other instruments . . . no trumpets, no drums, no clarinets, no trombones. I'm thinking this is what Butch meant when he asked you if you knew what you were getting into. We want you to create a band and hope the community will support it in addition to our choral program."

When all the questions had been voiced, Jake was asked to leave the room while the board members contemplated whether to offer him a contract. It took only five minutes. Upon returning to the board room, Don speaks profoundly.

"Jake, do you want to be our Professor of Music?"

"Yes!" was Jake's reply. A contract was signed for teaching band, orchestra, and voice. Jake walked out of the old school building realizing he had taken on another challenge, most likely bigger than any before. He was now the instructor of the St. John high school phantom band.

As summer waned and the first day of school drew near, Jake began to settle into his new community. The word on the street about him was mixed. "Does this young man know anything about music?" "Can he direct a band or teach our kids to march?" "Can he be a positive influence for our children and youth?" The jury was out as these questions lingered on the lips of the community. Jake was ready to render a verdict.

The St. John News, the town's weekly newspaper, was most supportive of Jake's presence in the community. The front page article read:

> All school students who are interested in belonging to the school band and orchestra next winter are asked to register at the high school building some time Friday or

## Knees Lifted High and Toes Pointed

> Saturday of this week. J.J. Dalke, who has been employed to take charge of the high school band, is planning to give free individual lessons to all students who are interested in doing instrument work for the remainder of the summer. He would like to get his practice schedule worked out as soon as possible. Any student who cares to learn to play an instrument should enroll whether he has an instrument at present or not. These free lessons are open to any boy or girl. As it is probable that there will be considerable demand for band and orchestra instruments, it is hoped that any persons in the community who have good band instruments for sale will list them with Mr. Dalke or with Supt. Don Kitch.

Classes began with thirty-five students ready to learn to play instruments or develop drum cadences. Each time Jake lifted his baton to direct, he could feel the surge of adrenaline and passion pouring forth. He had made the right decision. He belonged in this place. The year was 1934.

# CHAPTER 2

# Positivity

*(working with an upbeat attitude and doing one's best)*

# and Decency

Sweat trickled down his ruddy cheeks as Jake energetically directed his protégés, counting out loud, offering encouraging gestures. Many days the three oscillating fans were no match for the intense Kansas heat that poured through the open windows of the band room. The days were reminiscent of the scorching sun that bore down on a youthful Jake as he directed a team of horses through the furrows of the earth, keeping them on task, preparing the ground for planting. He learned early on the dynamics of teamwork. It was no different now, except he had a baton in his hand, not two long narrow leather straps attached to a bit. This was his team, made up of unique individuals, happily yoked and pulling together, with each young person drawing from his or her background, talent and energy for the good of the whole team. They were marching down the musical furrows, playing their trumpets, trombones, flutes, tubas, drums, clarinets, and cymbals.

Jake knew he could teach the value of music to any willing student. He had the knowledge. He had the intelligence. He certainly had the skills, knowing how to play all the instruments. Jake also knew that those qualities would not be enough. The missing ingredient for any budding musician was an extraordinary attitude. When Bobbie chose to play the bassoon, Jake knew he could teach her—the willingness to learn and excel was up to her—wrapped and bound in attitude. When Donny told Mr. Dalke that he wanted to play the baritone, his desire to learn bubbled over from a child-like enthusiasm and spilled into his spirited attitude. Donny would succeed and cherish a monumental moment in his life five years later. He played a melodic solo in the midst of the national band contest, causing the angels to savor his every note.

The banner on the music room wall read: **"We can make music!"** A positive attitude prevailed at every practice, as Jake would walk briskly to his music stand, make a few announcements and then raise his baton for a lively Sousa march. The school board had made the right decision. Jake remembered the powerful words of Don Kitch in accepting the signed contract:

> Jake, I like your spirit. That's why I want you for this job. But, let me tell you something—you need to be more than a music teacher to these kids. You also need to be their spiritual leader, not in the religious sense, but leading by example. Everyone around here is in a deep freeze. We have been battered by crop failures and stores shutting down. When Gray's Office Supply closed, you would have thought the whole town had collapsed. Those students you are teaching walk long distances to school in terrible conditions. Their parents kiss them goodbye each morning and send them to us. Do you know what kind of responsibility we have to not only teach, but offer them something beyond their education? That is why you are here. Jake, I've been here five years, and I haven't seen anything yet to lift the hopes of some of these students and their parents, except a one-point victory last year on the football field. There is one last thing: I am in your corner. You can count on me.

## POSITIVITY AND DECENCY

This powerful message rang each day in Jake's mind and heart as he smiled his way through sour notes, missed entrances and grimaced faces. He knew the best was yet to come for these young struggling musicians.

It was late in the school year that an invitation from radio station KFBK, several hundred miles away, asked if this new group of instrumentalists would be willing to present a program on a Sunday afternoon. The band was two years old. Already it was being recognized beyond St. John for its musical abilities. Let's call it believing in new possibilities. Let's call it walking on paths never before touched. Let's call it sixteen carloads of parents and their kids recognizing the truth of their banner, **"We can make music!"** Let's call it attitude.

Mr. Dalke had asked band members to wear their dark pants and white shirts for the radio broadcast. This decision did not make much sense to many of the students. Jimmy spoke up.

"Several of us have been wondering why we should dress up for a radio broadcast, where we will be sitting in a room with no audience. Who will see us?"

Jake's reply was classic.

"You will play your best when you look your best."

A positive attitude is one of the hallmarks of decency. It is reaching out to others with genuineness and caring. It is just not only understanding, but standing under. Picture the Armstrong family. Velma is preparing supper for her husband Calvin and their two teenage daughters, Charlene and Cleo. There are only three African American families living in St. John. The Armstrongs are one of them.

They are a modest family, having moved to the community three years ago, hoping to find a group of folks who would accept them amidst the heavy racial tensions throughout the country. Calvin, who owns his cobbler shop, is a pleasant soul. Velma, a stay-at-home mom, exudes protectiveness and love towards her family, especially her two daughters. Calvin begins to read out loud from the local newspaper.

## Knees Lifted High and Toes Pointed

"The high school band is coming along fine, and the youngsters are taking a real interest in it. Mr Dalke has the knack of getting work out of those who are studying music under him. Membership in the band is growing, but Mr. Dalke welcomes any young person who wants to learn to play an instrument or drum to contact him through the school office. Lessons will be free."

Calvin slowly looks up from the newspaper article.

"Hey, Cleo, Charlene. Would the two of you like to play in the band?"

The girls jump from their chairs and whoop with delight. In unison they respond, "Yes... yes... yes!"

Horrified that Calvin would suggest such a thing, Velma shoots him a *look* that leaves no doubt how she feels about her husband's suggestion. As the evening wears on, Velma and Calvin retreat to their bedroom for a night's rest. Taking a deep breath to calm her anger and concern, she says,

"Calvin, what makes you think our girls will be allowed to even try out for the band? You have set them up for disappointment. What are you thinking?"

Calvin responds, calmly.

"Well, they won't know until they try."

Velma continues to glare at Calvin:

> Don't you realize how much this will hurt them? In so many subtle ways they already feel shut out around here. They can't even go to the drugstore without being stared at, and when they do go in they sit in the farthest booth in the corner. We both know you wanted to leave the South and move to a small town in the Midwest so you could establish your business. You are great at what you do, probably because no one around here knows anything about fixing worn-out shoes. We both know it has not been easy. We have paid a price. We barely have friends. We don't dare eat out. We are politely tolerated most of the time. Tell me, why would you want to give Cleo and Charlene one more reason to feel different?

## Positivity and Decency

It is Saturday morning. Jake is pulling down some extra instruments from the shelves and shining them in case more students show interest and might want to take lessons. There is a knock on the band door. He greets the Armstrong family. After listening sensitively to their concerns, he begins to show the girls each instrument, demonstrating their sounds. Velma, with a cautious nod of approval to her husband, says,

"Mr. Dalke, when can the girls begin taking lessons?"

Looking directly at Charlene and Cleo, Jake replies,

"Let's start next week with your lessons. I'll place both of you in the beginner's band for now. When you learn to play your horns, you can move up to the concert band, and begin traveling to the surrounding towns."

What was there about Jake that reached out to this family with such compassion and understanding? His attitude was *I will support you*. He knew there would likely be band trips where Cleo and Charlene would not be allowed in restaurants or restrooms. Later he heard Katherine say,

"Jake, they can always ride with me. I will pack their lunches. We will do our best to stand under Cleo and Charlene."

Before the school year ended, band contests were being held throughout the area. The year before, Jake had traveled with four of his senior leaders to Phillips University in Enid, Oklahoma to observe its band festival. *Would the St. John band be able to compete? What would be the expectations of the judges? Should I accept an invitation to join the festival?. Was this the year to support the desires of many townsfolk, parents, and band members and enter the contest at Phillips University?*

A letter came from a band parent expressing the importance of attitude:

> Dear Mr. Dalke:
>
> It is almost impossible for me to come and tell you how much I appreciate your instructive ability, so I am writing instead. You have a wonderful command of your band and voice classes. I heard them earlier and lately. I am not much of a musician and only had one

year in rudiments of music, but I can appreciate what I hear. Dale has kept me pretty well informed along lots of things, and I believe I'd know you in the dark. It's Mr. Dalke this and Mr. Dalke that. I thank you for taking an interest in Dale. I don't believe you will ever regret it. Dale will work more for you than anyone I have known. So, make the most of him. He likes his band and voice class so much. Thank you for your interest in personal and public betterment. Sincerely,
Freeda Lilendorf.

## CHAPTER 3

# Patience

*❧ (continuing calmness and hope over time) ❧*

# and Decency

"Left, right, left, right, left, right, lift those knees high, point those toes." Every morning before classes began, the sound of Jake's voice and the nearly flawless footsteps of seventy-five eager band members marching on Main Street echoed throughout the community, especially for those who lived near the town square. George Soden said he would rise early and, with coffee cup in hand, perch himself on the curb of the wide brick streets and just watch and listen. He called it his "Stars and Stripes Forever" wake up call.

In St. John there were several activities for young people to do besides school. Available were the 4-H Club, a city recreation center for dancing and ping-pong, a pond outside of town for winter ice skating, and church activities. In addition schools became the focal point of life in the community, with a few clubs, vocal groups, and of course athletics. But now, there was a new sound in town.

## Knees Lifted High and Toes Pointed

The band was growing in numbers. Its reputation was building, and invitations to play in parades and give concerts on a regular basis for the hometown fans were sorely needed and deeply appreciated. Folks were coming to football games to witness the halftime performances, full of creativity and patriotic themes. In contrast, the team was struggling.

> **ST. JOHN WAS AGAIN BEATEN**
>
> For the Ninth Consecutive Year the Tigers Have Been Victims of Stafford in Turkey Day Game.—Better Game Than Score Indicates.
>
> (By Winford Broadfoot)
> The Stafford high school football team added another Turkey Day victory to its already long string, when they defeated, probably their keenest rival, the St. John high school football team by a score of 19 to 6, Thursday, Nov. 29, on a snow and ice-crested gridiron at Stafford.
>
> **Stafford Scored First**
> An alert Stafford team was the first to score; in fact scoring a touchdown on their first offensive play of the game, after a St. John back had fumbled the opening kick-off on his own 2-yard line and a Stafford gridster recovered for Stafford at that point. Brock, Stafford's star player, then went through the line for the extra point to give his team a 7 to 0 lead in the first few seconds of the game.
>
> Shortly after the half, Brock again

The band was surpassing all expectations. The students were enthralled with attention from the local newspaper and jubilant talk on the street. The superintendent of Stafford County schools took the time to write J.J. Dalke and the St. John Band:

> I just want to tell you how much I enjoyed your concert Tuesday night. There was evidence of real program-building and enough variety to suit every taste. It was colorful, too. The novelties, I think are the best I ever heard at a band concert. The fact is, I have heard professional concerts at higher prices that did not give me any more satisfaction than the concert you played. I wish to congratulate you upon the progress you are making and assure you of my best wishes and

cooperation. You are making a real contribution to the life of our community.
Sincerely yours,
Ralph Edwards

Jake knew the future was promising. He also knew there is a fine line between being enthusiastic and being overly so. He needed to temper his excitement with patience. After the wheat had been planted on the family farm, his dad, mom and seven siblings could only pray for the right amount of rain and sunshine before a hopeful harvest. As his dad would say,

"We must all have patience. The rain will come in due time, and the sun will shine when it wants. All we can do is till the ground and plant the seed. That's all we can do, and then we will harvest!"

Clanging pans, exhilarating shouts from revelers and loud party gatherings greeted the new year. Jake knew 1936 could be pivotal for the band, but he had to lead eagerly within realistic expectations. He was also directing the high school orchestra, which included many of his band members. They were rehearsing diligently on Schubert's *Symphony Suite*, which had four movements, no less. It was a very difficult piece of music. He believed the students could learn it for the concert to be given during the second semester. Everyone needed to practice their music with patience. He just wanted to provide the opportunity for his students to stretch their newly-found talents and, most of all, to have fun.

Those Saturday evening concerts in the park were just what the community—and the band—needed. It was a time of frivolity, and feeding one's senses. People came from all parts of town and the county. The benches began to fill and cars arrived early to take the prime parking places around the square. Windows were rolled down to allow the music to soak in. Children played on the grass and did tricks on the blankets placed near the makeshift stage. Don Kitch always introduced the band with special attention given to Jake.

"Good evening, on this pleasant summer evening. Once again I am most happy to welcome all of you to our concert in the park. I give you our high school concert band, under the highly capable direction of Jake Dalke."

Applause broke out. Car horns honked their approval. Another rousing program, with two encores, penetrated the warm summer air.

Daily the concert band was preparing for their most challenging performance to date. It was not unexpected for the St. John News to tout the band as being one of the very best, if not the best, high school band in Kansas. Jake knew that was a small exaggeration spiced with hometown pride. Band news often usurped the headlines from local politics, school athletics, and deaths in the community. As one might imagine, the lack of publicity or negative publicity strongly irritated the coaches. Conflict was brewing.

A newspaper article began:

"Professor Dalke's celebrated high school band will give one of its very pleasing and entertaining concerts Tuesday night in Convention Hall. A splendid program has been arranged. An overflowing house is expected and it would be advisable to secure reserved seats early through Haas Jewelry Store."

Confidence in the band's abilities was continuing to grow. How well Jake remembered those fledgling years when he scheduled a concert in convention hall, five months after sixty-five kids began playing instruments for the first time.

"This is your reward for willingness to learn." It was also a time to raise money for band uniforms.

"You are a band. You play like a band. But, we don't look like a band."

He had been cautiously patient.

Jake was continually receiving calls from parents and members of the Chamber of Commerce suggesting the band was good enough to enter marching and concert contests in the area. Decisions were on the horizon. Jake knew notoriety was not only contagious but could lead to making hasty choices that might not lead to positive outcomes for the present or the future. The inner voice that spoke so long ago was speaking again. It was the quiet whisper of wisdom—be patient.

# Chapter 4

# Humility

*◦◦ (selfless service with no sense of entitlement) ◦◦*

# and Decency

"Hey, sissy Dalke!"

One of Jake's strongest beliefs was that everyone deserved to be treated equally, especially his band members. His philosophy was fourfold: 1) we are all created as unique human beings, 2) no one deserves special privileges or treatment, 3) we learn how to live through hard times and make the best of difficult relationships, and 4) we must not live our lives at the expense of others. He modeled these principles and expected no less from his students.

He recognized the voice from the second story window. It was one of his trumpet players. Without looking up or saying a word, Jake walked determinedly to the second floor classroom. Students were gathered around the windows, shouting distasteful and sarcastic comments to classmates entering the building. As he opened the door, everyone became quiet and nervously attentive. Looking at Charlie, he said,

"I heard what you said to me. Sissy is a word we do not use in my band, or in this school. I will not tolerate that kind of name-calling. When you make fun of another person, it only tears you down. It doesn't make you popular or a hero to your classmates. Am I clear?"

Tears welled up in Charlie's eyes. The room was eerily quiet as he spoke to Mr. Dalke.

"I'm sorry. I won't do it again."

"Charlie," said Jake, "I don't want you to make fun of anyone ever again, especially your classmates. This band needs you. You are a fine trumpet player. We can also go to parades and contests without you—if this behavior continues. Am I clear?"

The word spread that day throughout the school. Mr. Dalke meant business in how we were to treat one another. There was no entitlement in his band. And what he asked of each band member he also asked of himself. When he said "yes" to accepting the position of Professor of Music, he knew this little community was a conglomeration of survivors, and his potential band members would represent all walks of life. He knew his success depended on his willingness to live out the strong values of his faith. He would accept each family for who they were. They were different from each other but could pull together. Yes, the Copelands, Radkeys, Kelchs, and the Armstrongs living together in harmony but not at one another's expense.

Saturdays in small towns often include settling public business over cups of fresh-brewed coffee in a main street café. Giving credence to feelings expressed by the old phrase *the best of friends are two people who dislike the same person* underscores much of the conversation. Often there is a false sense of superiority in demeaning others who don't meet the expectations of the coffee klatch *majority*.

This day, Frank, and several of the locals, have gathered for breakfast and conversation at the café on the square. Some of them have their WWI caps on, depicting the sections of the military in which they served. They range in age from forty-five to seventy.

Cigarette and pipe smoke adds a layer of cloudiness, as they all sit closely around a table.

"Well, boys," says Frank sarcastically, "we are off to another great season. Think we will win a game? I'll tell you one thing, if we don't beat Greensburg on Thanksgiving Day, you can count on this season being one of the worst we've seen around these parts in recent times."

Frank, who believes himself to be the voice of reason, continues to speak.

"Those boys would be better off carrying a rifle than a football."

Jake walks in, sits at the counter, and orders a cup of coffee. He opens the newspaper and alternately carries on a conversation with the waitress while reading the sports page. As he turns a page, he notices a table of men across the room and becomes aware of their loud and boisterous voices. A couple of the men also notice Jake. One of the old-timers speaks loud enough for him to hear.

"I've lived here all my life, except the war years. The one thing I've always looked forward to is Friday night or Saturday afternoon at Brown Athletic Field. Hard-nose hitting. The cracking of helmets. And no silly band, either. Leave that music stuff to the big schools in Wichita or Topeka. Those horns cost too much, and we ain't got enough money in this town as it is."

Jake keeps listening to the conversation but does not acknowledge it. Once again it is Frank's turn to prophesy. Looking up and down the table at the "prognosticators of truth", Frank leans forward to emphasize his point.

"I hear some of our local boys are going to enlist. They need to protect our country. I mean, one more year and we'll be in war again. Won't be anything like what we faced. It was a nightmare—those ugly, loud German tanks and poison gases. We are lucky to be sitting here right now."

Frank jumps in again. "Dalke... now that's a German name, ain't it? We probably fought some of his people. You know, it's too bad girls can't enlist. Except those Armstrong kids would be too chicken to ship out."

## Knees Lifted High and Toes Pointed

Jake folds his newspaper, lays a coin on the counter, and walks slowly out of the café with a heavy heart. He believes no one is entitled to make fun of, condemn, or degrade another person. He does not tolerate that kind of behavior in his band. The negativity of the beliefs and judgements expressed at the café and spoken with such conviction are not for him to deal with at this time.

His energy shifts towards calling a special band practice to polish their halftime routine, to find their positions on the field, and to play from memory. He knows his selection, "When Johnny Comes Marching Home," will likely elicit a number of sentimental responses, from prayerful folks of all ages to veterans standing with their hands over their hearts. However, what he observed in the café causes him unrest and fear. He asks himself, *Can music inspire this community to think and feel differently about their lives?*

The next morning several young men, duffels slung over their shoulders, tearfully hug their loved ones and friends as they board the train. The band stands in formation near the train platform and plays, "The Caissons Go Rolling Along" and "From the Halls of Montezuma." The train slowly pulls away. The band softly plays a hymn.

# CHAPTER 5

# Adversity

*(life can sometimes be calamitous)*

# and Decency

Two episodes weren't tragic, well—one of them could have been—but they reminded Jake how tenuous the band's success was.

### ENID, OKLAHOMA

For the past two and one-half years he and the band had received accolades for accomplishing the impossible. And now it was off to Phillips University in Enid, Oklahoma, to play in one of the nation's premier concert and marching contests. Jake and a few of his band members had scouted the venue twelve months previously. This year they received an invitation to participate. They knew it would be a learning experience regardless of how they placed in the rankings.

Only a handful of the band kids had ever been to a college campus. What an exciting experience awaited them! After the instruments, music stands and eighty "giddy" musicians were loaded into the cars and pickups, the caravan headed south out of St. John. Katherine's dad, John, had volunteered to be one of the drivers. That particular day the wind was strong, and once again the dust and sand limited the driver's vision to a maximum speed of forty-five miles per hour. Twenty minutes from home, an unusually strong gust of wind jarred John's car sideways, causing the front tire to catch the edge of the road. As he struggled to pull the car back onto the pavement, the skidding vehicle lunged towards a culvert and rolled over on its side, looking like a tin casket with slowly rotating wheels. Jake and Katherine, who were coming along directly behind the accident, quickly stopped in panic and disbelief.

Other drivers and nattily-uniformed band members stopped and began looking through shattered windows, prying open doors, and talking to the kids and John. Fortunately, no one was seriously injured, except for an ample amount of cuts and bruises. Katherine insisted on taking everyone to the nearest hospital emergency room, located in Medicine Lodge.

As the injured were being helped into a vacated car serving as the makeshift ambulance, Jake pulled Katherine aside and said,

"This is awful. I feel so badly. I'm grateful no one is seriously hurt. I know this is our first opportunity to attend a band festival, but do you think we should call off the trip?"

For a moment Katherine hesitated. There was a strong part of her that wanted to say *Yes, I think we should turn around and go back to St. John. Nothing is more important than the health of these injured kids or my dad.* Instead, she responded,

"You need to go on with the rest of the band. I have the situation in hand. Don't worry. I'm so sorry this happened."

The procession of cars continued to Enid.

The curtain was closed. The band sat poised on the stage. Over the public address system boomed the announcement:

> Ladies and gentlemen, and students. On the way to Enid, the St. John Band encountered an unfortunate accident. A carload of students and their driver slid off the road

and rolled once in a dusty field. We understand they were taken to a nearby hospital and are resting well at this time. Indeed, we are very sorry for the accident and wish them well in their recovery. The rest of the band elected to continue their trip, and so at this time let's all welcome the St. John, Kansas high school band, under the direction of Mr. Jake Dalke.

Applause erupted throughout the auditorium. The curtain opened with a flare, and Jake walked briskly to the front of his group, bowed to the audience, and turned to face his young musicians. Just as he raised his baton, several students emerged from the side of the stage with spots of dried blood on their uniforms and bandages around their foreheads and hands. Prolonged clapping increased in volume. Jake turned to face the crowd once again. This time, however, he pulled away from the center of the stage and gestured for the band to stand. They had not made one musical sound. They didn't have to.

The music they played that day was incidental to the courage expressed on the stage. Katherine, standing by her dad, watched from the side of the pulled curtain as Jake visibly coped to direct; he was overcome with emotion. In spite of a near tragedy, the band placed first in concert and first in marching.

The next day, Jake addressed the band. Tapping his music stand, he began to speak.

"We . . . we did it! We went to our first festival. I am so grateful everyone is safe and healing. That is much more important than bringing home trophies for first place in concert and marching. Thank you . . . I'm just grateful for all of you. We have overcome adversity. Now we march at the game this Friday night. Here is your practice schedule. We need to memorize our music. I know I am asking a lot from each of you. But don't neglect your homework!"

## JAKE AND THE COACHES

The scoreboard flashed: Claflin 21 – St. John 0. The football team was on a losing streak, which didn't please the patrons of the community. In contrast, the enthusiastic praise for the band's performances throughout the state only served to irritate the coaches. It was halftime and the team walked off the playing field, weaving their way through the musicians who were getting into position to lift their knees high and point their toes. The public address announcer boomed,

"And now, it is my pleasure to present the best band in the state of Kansas, the St. John Tiger marching band!"

As he followed his team from the playing field, Coach Morrison glared at Jake. The air was stagnant and the odor of sweat permeated the locker room. Hanging on the wall were the words:

## "ONLY SISSIES GIVE UP – WHO ARE YOU?"

The game ended with another loss for the floundering team. Coach Morrison and his assistant, Mike, were feeling the pressure to win. They also resented that the talk on the street was two-fold— the wonderful success of the band and the lousy job the coaches were doing with the football team. It was time to have a talk with Don Kitch, who was instrumental in hiring Jake.

"Come in," bellows Don, his voice matching the intensity of the boisterous knock on his door. Hank and Mike take seats in front of Don's desk, their arms crossed, their faces tense. Don breaks the silence.

"I understand you still are concerned about the progress of the band, and that it could affect some of your players who want to play in the band and play football. Is this right?"

Mike jumps in.

"Well, we just don't think there is a place in this little town for two strong programs. What we want you to do . . . "

"Hang on, Mike," says Coach Morrison:

> Let me spell it all out. Football has been here long before any music program. And football is here to stay. You know how important winning is to this town. It makes people happy. They look forward to Friday nights. But Don, you and I both know we would have done better this year if some of my best players had not spent so much time

marching and practicing their . . . er . . . whatever they do. Come on, Don. You know what's right. I say, let the kids play their horns at church or in their homes, but the truth is, Jake Dalke is a distraction. Everyone knows that!

Don listens, well aware the coaches are fighting for their jobs. The townsfolk are sick and tired of losing. The band has brought new energy to the community, and the expectations for the band are far-reaching.

"I understand your upset feelings. I want to bring Jake into this conversation. I believe he is in the band room. I'll send for him. Just stay seated."

Jake grew up believing adversity and conflict need to be confronted and worked through to the benefit of everyone involved. Sitting in Don's office with two hostile and antagonistic faculty members could be one of Jake's biggest challenges. He enters the room.

"Sit down, Jake," Don says.

"Coach Morrison and Coach Mike feel like the band is competing with the football program, and they are losing support of the town. I'd like for you to respond to them."

Jake is thoughtful with his words, but his feelings are bouncing around like a fumbled football. With his pronounced German accent he looks directly at both coaches and says:

> I am not, hear me, not competing with your football program. I have never said, nor will I say, one program is more important than another. This school needs a strong athletic program and a strong music program. We can work together. No one has to feel pulled. In college I was the starting quarterback on the football team and at the same time majored in music. I also sang in a traveling quartet. If one of your players wants to learn how to play an instrument, I will not deny giving him lessons. I will also encourage him to do his best on the football field, and when he is able, to do his best on the concert stage and marching in the band. It can be worked out.

## Knees Lifted High and Toes Pointed

The message seemed clear to the coaches. As long as Don Kitch was the superintendent, Jake's position was secure, and theirs wasn't. Little did they know that within the year Don would be leaving to take a position in California. The new superintendent, Emmett Jennings, an overzealous supporter of athletic programs in the schools, would be hired. Jake's belief in positively embracing the dynamics of adversity was yet to be challenged.

## CHAPTER 6

# TRUST

*(emotional security in relationships)*

# AND DECENCY

"THE TWO COLOREDS CANNOT SIT with the rest of your group. Let me take them to a section in the back of the restaurant."

The words cut like a serrated knife. The band members stood motionless. Jake started to step forward, only to have Katherine say,

"Let me handle this."

Cleo and Charlene, well aware of what had just taken place, stared down at their shoes, humiliated and a bit frightened. Katherine pulled the middle-aged, well-dressed manageress aside, and spoke precisely.

"I will be dining with these two young ladies. Please show the rest of the children to their seats." Her response unmistakably expressed decency.

Not giving the hostess a chance to respond, Katherine swooped Cleo and Charlene from the group, took them by their hands, and proceeded to the segregated area in the back of the dining hall. They sat down, nervously looking at the menu.

In the middle of fall concert preparations and exciting half-time shows at football games, Jake received an invitation for his band to appear at the American Royal Stock Show in Kansas City. This elite event drew ranchers, farmers and interested people from several states. Indeed, it was an honor for the band to receive this invitation. This was the first major occasion with regional significance that was not a festival. The band would be noticed as never before, as they would march through the business district of Kansas City in the afternoon and play in the stock show arena that evening. A special train car was chartered. The cost was $4 round trip.

The old WWI cannon sounded its blast, and the parade began. Bands from all over the country began marching in front of dignitaries and esteemed groups of United States Congressmen and Congresswomen. St. John was seventh in line. Jake had taught his fine musicians the political campaign tunes for that year. One of his strengths was choosing music to fit every occasion. "Oh, Susanna" pleased all the Republicans, and "Sidewalks of New York" created a stir with the Democrats. Regardless of political persuasion, the thousands lining the streets gave the band a loud ovation. Congressman U.S. Guyer was so impressed he jumped from the platform and walked two blocks alongside the St. John band. As he left them, he flashed a huge smile, shook Jake's hand, and saluted the young musicians.

At the end of the parade route the thirty-nine bands were picked up by street cars and escorted to the American Royal Building. Each band was given twenty minutes to do its marching maneuvers and play music of its choice. The lights were lowered as the band bowed their heads in readiness. As the lights of the arena came up, so did the instruments, with a sound swelling and filling the whole building. Prompted by a snappy cadence from the drums, the band broke into a quick march step. Horns were held exactly at the same level. The show was on.

One maneuver after another, all choreographed to the rhythm of the music, brought the crowd to its feet. In climactic fashion, the band paused, and upon command from their drum major, who shouted a new cadence, the band began to march to three-quarter time, as they played the "Missouri Waltz." Cheers erupted from the crowd, and people jumped to their feet, waving hats and handkerchiefs. The music ended. The band bowed in unison. It was time to get a good night's rest and return home.

The trip for the band was marred once again by the painful incident of inequality. When the St. John News heard what happened, their headline read, "Band Takes Giant Step Towards Recognition and Equality." While it was a step towards future contests, and possible national recognition, it was more than that. It was respect for human decency.

Summer was over. Fluttering leaves welcomed the fall term. It was fall, 1938.

*We have a musical mountain to climb, and I must lead them to the top.* These words had rung inside Jake's head from the time he said yes to the job offer in 1934, to each eager step he took into the band room. He knew what to do. He knew how to do it. He knew he couldn't do it alone. He would need the support and respect of the school board, the parents of the band kids, the band mothers club, the townsfolk, and most of all, the young people who put instruments to their lips or drum sticks in their hand.

Trusting relationships do not happen overnight. It had taken three years of honesty and straight talk to develop a *crack* marching band as the St. John News described the musical organization. Young musicians' words echoed up and down the halls of the school. "Mr. Dalke can get us to do anything."

The onset of the new school term brought many invitations for the band to perform. Tops on their list was the opportunity to march at the Kansas State Fair. Only a few bands were selected for this exciting annual event. Jake's group, now eighty-five strong, captured the attention of fairgoers with their snappy footwork and enthusiastic playing. As he marched beside the band, he thought, *If these kids only knew. All I want is for the community and parents to trust me and have confidence in my teaching and ability to cultivate the character of these innocent young people. I just need everyone on board.*

Every few months Will Rogers came to St. John. Oh, not in person, but on the screen. Sadly, he had died a few years earlier in a plane crash near Point Barrow, Alaska. His homespun witticisms gave hope to many people caught in the depressed times. The Deluxe Theater's advertisement went something like this: "We are proud to present the star who shall never be forgotten. He's always made you laugh . . . sometimes made you sob. But, never have you seen him in a role so rich in human emotion . . . as in this stirring romance of the old Mississippi."

In the 1930s young and old needed to hang on to messages of hope. They needed to trust in things tangible and intangible. World War I, which was waged until the early 1920s, was still affecting some families who lived in fear of more war and loss of human life. As the 1930s began, the United States plunged into the Great Depression, and didn't crawl out of it until 1940. Humorists like Will Rogers, political figures, preachers, and newspaper columnists provided the inspiration for anxious people to carry on. Survival was constantly being challenged. Economic life was threatened by lack of jobs. Machines stood idle. People, like those in St. John, became vulnerable to follow anyone who had an answer for the ills of society.

Will Rogers was dead. His messages would live on, but it was up to young and old alike to pull inside themselves and believe in their own goodness and ability to make the best of every situation regardless of the national or local circumstances.

What were the messages of hope? Where could people turn? Certainly, organized religion tried to offer direction and comfort. The Bible quotes Jesus as saying, "Lo, I am with you always, even to the ends of the earth." That was a comforting scripture for the believer. But, buried deeply inside many business people, farmers, and moms and dads, was the need for a sense of community—a way to pull together—and music was becoming the common denominator for the St. John townsfolk. The band symbolized new beginnings. The young musicians learned to play while a country struggled to survive. There was a catchy buoyancy in their marching when many in the community were in low spirits. The young people smiled while sadness was the prevailing feeling amongst many of the townsfolk. They awakened the hearts of people that wanted to sleep because it was hard to have energy or belief that tomorrow would be a better day.

Jake began seriously contemplating getting the band ready for a national contest in Omaha, Nebraska. Several barriers had to be crossed before any plans could be considered. First, the band had to qualify at the upcoming district festival in Pratt, Kansas by receiving a highly superior rating. Second, there was the matter of money. How could the band members and their chaperones afford such a long trip, which would involve several days of food and lodging?

After two days of music and marching, the district festival concluded. St. John High School Band received the highest honor afforded any band. In addition to noting their musical skills, the Pratt Daily Tribune also printed the following:

"The St. John band was perhaps the most outstandingly uniformed. Their new blue coats, white trousers and military caps gave the young bandsmen a trim appearance."

Local business owners, the Chamber of Commerce, and interested band boosters voted unanimously to offer financial backing for the trip to Omaha. Jake knew the time was ripe for his musicians to test the music scene nationally. Until this year, they were not ready even though the town had cheered them with honking horns for the past four years, believing they were the greatest. Jake knew the time was right. The community, parents, and band members trusted his judgment. It was time to load the buses for Omaha.

Yes, Will was dead, but the band was vibrantly alive.

## CHAPTER 7

# Making Room

*(honoring all people)*

# and Decency

THE BANNER AT THE HOTEL headquarters read: "Welcome To The National Music Festival." A much smaller sign on the side of the Santa Fe Trailways buses simply read:

"St. John, Kansas Tiger Marching Band."

Momentum was building in the racing hearts of each band member. Many had tucked in their suitcases the write-up from the St. John News, which read:

> They're off for Omaha, National Music Festival, Omaha, Nebraska. The St. John High School Band won the right to compete in the National Music Festival at Omaha by scoring a Highly Superior rating in the District Music Festival in Pratt, April 16-17. St. John merchants, professional men and individuals have cooperated wholeheartedly with J.J. Dalke and members of the band, and their combined efforts have made this trip possible. St. John is proud of its band, as rightly it should be. St. John High School's crack band left this Thursday morning

for Omaha in two Santa Fe Trailways buses, chartered for the purpose, and four cars. The trip was expected to be completed by tonight, and the band concert is scheduled for tomorrow, Friday morning. Friday evening the marching contest will be held. Enroute home the band will stop at Lincoln, Nebraska, Capital of the state, where they will have an opportunity to see the famous Nebraska Capitol building, acknowledged to be one of the finest in the country.

Students from Missouri, Kansas, Colorado, Wyoming, Nebraska, Iowa and South Dakota checked into the hotel. There were 16 marching bands. It was an overwhelming experience to just mingle in the hotel lobby. Jake proceeded to register at the contestant headquarters.

"I'm Jake Dalke from St. John, Kansas. I believe we have reservations for ninety-six people for three days."

The clerk fumbled through the papers on the counter. Taking a deep breath, he shuffled through many sets of papers and reservations. Scratching his head, he motioned to another clerk, and they began speaking in low tones.

"Mr. Dalke, when did you make the reservations?"

"They were made four weeks ago, right after we found out we would be coming here to play in the contest. Is there a problem?"

"Well, yes. There is a big problem. We apparently have lost your reservation. And, as you might imagine, we are sold out for the next three nights due to the music contest. I'm very sorry, but there is nothing we can do. There is an old hotel outside of town you might check with, but I usually don't recommend it."

Jake, panicked and deeply frustrated, walked towards Katherine, pulling her away from the band kids.

"They lost our reservations. And the hotel is full for the next three nights. This is horrible. I'm going to call the manager of this place and demand he find us rooms. If that doesn't work, we will have to sleep on the floor and dress on the buses. These kids need to be rested and ready to go in the morning. In my wildest dreams I wouldn't have guessed this would happen to us."

## Making Room and Decency

Looking at his pocket watch, he noticed the hour is now 7 p.m. The kids haven't eaten, and most of them are very tired from the trip. Katherine speaks with a measure of compassionate authority.

"Jake, leave it all to me. You are tired. Go sit down. Close your eyes and try to relax."

Katherine moves towards the hotel clerk.

"I need an extra telephone and a directory, plus a private place where I can make a few notes."

Knowing the urgency of the situation, the clerk responds quickly. Time passes. The large clock in the hotel lobby chimes 8:30 p.m. Katherine jostles Jake by the shoulder and says,

"Help me round up the kids. Everything has been worked out."

With a sigh of relief, Jake announces to the band they will be staying in private homes near the downtown area. Their hosts are on the way. Cleo and Charlene anxiously look at each other.

As the last car leaves the hotel with the four remaining band members, Jake looks into Katherine's eyes with gratitude and amazement.

"How did you do it?"

"It's a very long story involving a phone and a local directory and hopefully some very nice people. I'll tell you all about it someday when you are old and gray."

The trip, to this point, was an emphatic example of what it meant to make room for information and circumstances you did not anticipate. It was decency personified. It was avoiding the first impulse. It was the proverbial taking a deep breath before responding and problem-solving. And, there was more to come.

It was a new day. They were the second band to play that morning. The judges sat at their tables, tapping their pencils, as the St. John band played their two required concert numbers before a large audience. It was not one of their better performances. Tired, they missed notes and entrances, frowning whenever that happened. Jake slowly put his baton down on the podium and started to walk off the stage, offering a slight understanding smile to the band. One of the judges stood and said,

"Mr. Dalke, if you will please remain at the podium, we will give you your music for the sight-reading portion."

As he leans down to receive the scores there is great puzzlement on his face. A conversation ensues, with both men huddled closely to one another. Their visit is intense, and hushed.

"You know, this is a surprise to me," says Jake. "We weren't notified about doing any sight-reading. At districts there is not a sight-reading part of the competition. My band doesn't have the slightest idea what to do, and I'm not too sure myself."

The judge looks surprised.

"You weren't notified that this would be a major part of this competition?"

"No. Not a word. You know, this has not been too great a trip for us. They lost our hotel reservations. We stayed with people we'd never met, and now this . . . what do I do? I can't leave these kids stranded on the stage in front of everyone."

The judge had no choice but to proceed.

"Just go back to the podium. I will make an announcement and review the rules once again for the audience as to what this portion of the contest is about. Sorry for the mix-up. Good luck."

How do you make room for the unexpected? You just listen and do your best, which is what Jake and the band did. Jake had ten minutes to study the score and another eight minutes to present the piece to the band, pointing out difficult passages and explaining the dynamics of the number. The struggling young musicians sweat together through the unfamiliar piece. It was a humiliating experience.

Later that afternoon, they presented their marching routines in one of the high school stadiums. Their lines were uncharacteristically crooked. The musicians were tired.

Morning couldn't come fast enough for the band to board their buses and cars and head west to St. John. Before leaving, Jake gathered his tired musicians in the hotel lobby for one last word:

> This has been quite a trip. You behaved wonderfully, especially given all the circumstances. There is one thing I do not want you to forget. We might not have welcomed

every unusual and unexpected thing that came our way, but we made room for it and didn't let anything overcome us. We are taking home a second in concert and a third in marching. Of course, we didn't place in the sight-reading. Next year I know we will all be a lot wiser when it comes to these competitions.

The band arrived home at 2:15 a.m. At 7 a.m. Jake received a call from his good friend and loyal supporter, superintendent Don Kitch.

"Jake, I have resigned and will be moving to California. I understand a new superintendent has been hired."

## CHAPTER 8

# HUMOR

*⸙ (the treasure of mirth) ⸙*

# AND DECENCY

JAKE WAS SUBTLY HUMOROUS. Rarely did he tell a joke. It would be out of character for him to laugh so hard that tears might run down his roughened cheeks. He didn't believe in poking fun at others but could chuckle with them. Maybe it was his Mennonite upbringing. Ah, but he could tell a story that was full of humor about a life situation.

One such tale occurred with Elmer, a school board member who was riding in Jake's car on a hot summer day. He inadvertently sat on a melted Hershey bar, and when exiting the car, his beige pants looked as if he had . . . well, you can allow your imagination to complete the picture. That vivid incident was recounted in the family for years, with much enjoyment.

And who could forget Jake putting shaving cream instead of whipped cream on a delicious brownie and serving it to a talkative guest. He said,

"I thought it would keep him quiet for a while."

## Humor and Decency

Jake had a wily side to his personality, and it was often expressed in band rehearsals. Even though he may have been a tad naïve about youth vernacular, the students respected his thoughts and words. The message was clear: Mr. Dalke wanted his young people to be more than competent members of a well-known band. High on his list was an expectation for them to be good citizens and to take care of themselves spiritually, mentally, and physically. Often subtle humor was his way of expressing this message.

Peggy played first chair flute. She was very frail in appearance. Every practice Jake would raise his left hand to begin directing and invariably notice Peggy. Here was this waif of a human being, looking almost like the long slender instrument she held to her lips. In the middle of a rehearsal Jake put down his baton and stood in front of the startled flutist. He said,

"Do you drink milk?" Amazed, Peggy answered hesitantly.

"Uh, well, uh, sometimes."

Jake looked at her with intensity and said,

"You'd be stronger if you drank milk. When you go home tonight, you tell your folks to buy you some Bosco. Put two spoonfuls in your milk. Let me know tomorrow how you like it." He had a twinkle in his eye as he refocused on the music.

"Alright band, let's pick it up at measure seventeen."

The tuba section was a different story. Here were four robust young boys toting those huge brass sousaphones with big shiny bells towering overhead. They took pride in polishing these imposing instruments and swinging them back and forth when they marched. On this day, in the middle of the rehearsal, no one suspected what would fall out of the bell of Christopher's sousaphone—an almost empty whiskey bottle. He had hidden the bottle in his horn and forgotten about it. As he placed the instrument on the floor between numbers, the bottle rolled out and settled under the chairs of the trumpet section. Laughter broke out. The object of Carrie Nation's wrath had graced the rehearsal.

Jake approached the four young men, all blushing innocently. Everyone stopped laughing and watched Mr. Dalke as he picked up the bottle.

"Does this belong to all of you, or just one of you?"

There was a subtle bit of humor in Jake's words and expression. At first there was no reply. Jake continued.

"Are any of you drinking during our practices?"

Hesitantly but in unison, they replied, "No sir."

In that very moment, memories of all of Jake's high school and college escapades came crashing down upon him. He hadn't put whiskey bottles in his instruments, but he did, while on a college quartet trip, put a dead skunk under the hood of his car and asked the gas station attendant to check the oil. Another time he joined his buddies in squirting cold water on unaware young female sunbathers, who were enjoying the warm day on a second-floor dormitory balcony.

Jake paused, looked at the frightened young men, and with a huge smile said,

"I won't tell your parents. Now, throw it away, and let's get on with our rehearsal."

Jack was a trombonist. He chose to be in the band because Mr. Dalke was the director. He took private lessons because Mr. Dalke was his tutor. He attended the senior high Sunday school class at the Methodist Church because Mr. Dalke was the teacher. He really didn't care if he learned how to play the trombone as long as he had the opportunity to be around Mr. Dalke. He was heard to say,

"It's fun playing in the band. I love hanging around Mr. Dalke. I'm not real good, but I have enough smarts to not play when it comes to the hard parts." A huge grin accompanied his words.

Jake knew life had its serious moments too. When he was in his first year out of college, his father died. At that time the question presented itself to him once again. *Should I go back and help on the farm or apply for a teaching position miles from home?* Life was often complicated and the direction was not always clear. It was the same in the Armstrong home.

It is Sunday morning, and Velma, Calvin, Charlene and Cleo are seated around the kitchen table having breakfast. The girls are doing their best, rubbing their eyes and trying to be alert. Velma breaks the silence.

"I'm glad we didn't drive out in the country to go to church this morning. Sometimes I think the Lord forgives us for not making the effort. You girls have been so busy with your summer concerts in the park and all those parades. I'm sure you are happy to be back in school."

"I don't know, Mama," Charlene responds. "I heard Lisa talking the other day, and she said we might march in as many as fifteen parades. It's a lot of work, memorizing all that music. Mr. Dalke thinks we can concentrate better on what we are doing if we play from memory. He says it is easier to keep our lines straight. And, we will be playing several concerts, as well."

Cleo, who is slowly waking up, chimes in.

"I sure hope we do better at the next national band contest than we did in Omaha. That was the worst."

"Speaking of Omaha," Velma inquires. "You girls never did say how you got along. Any troubles like you had when you went to the American Royal in Kansas City?"

Charlene spoke quickly.

"Kansas City was embarrassing. If Mrs. Dalke hadn't been with us, no telling what would have happened. She wasn't about to let us sit alone in that dumb restaurant. Same way in Omaha, too. I think she maybe understands what we go through and doesn't like it."

Cleo speaks with gratefulness.

"Yeah, when our hotel rooms fell through, she just took over. Being in homes was kinda fun, but I sure was wondering where we would be staying."

"I don't think you ever said if you stayed with a black family, or not," said Calvin.

"Nope. The family we were with had two kids our age, and they were white as white can be . . . and nice, too. Wonder how Mrs. Dalke arranged that?"

Velma echoes Charlene's words.

## Knees Lifted High and Toes Pointed

"I will admit I was skeptical about the two of you joining the band. Maybe your daddy was right. It has been a good learning experience for both of you."

Cleo had been having thoughts about her future for the past several months, but she hadn't had the courage to voice them.

"I've decided when I graduate I want to go to college and learn to be a band director."

"You what?" exclaims Calvin.

"I said, when I graduate from high school, I want to go to college and learn to be a band director, like Mr. Dalke."

"And your daddy and I will support you a hundred percent, but first, just get out of high school, okay?"

Velma moves away from the table, quite satisfied with this Sunday morning's family discussion. *I didn't think it was possible to feel this way about their joining the band,* she says to herself.

There was something ironic about Cleo's dream for her future. It resembled her band director's dual approach to life's uncertainties, with both seriousness and humor. If only Jake knew!

# CHAPTER 9

# FLEXIBILITY

*(adapting well to changing circumstances)*

# AND DECENCY

THEY STOOD AT ATTENTION—all seven of them—their dad's voice booming.

"I need all of you kids in the field today. Looks like rain later, so put your baseball gloves and your sewing in your rooms, change your shoes and meet me outside in ten minutes. I know I promised you a day off, but this is the way it is. Now, get moving!"

Jake learned early on that life does not always unfold as hoped-for or planned. At times he had to take emotional and physical time-outs. He was flexible and modeled such for others. He had met the challenge of creating a band when there was not a band. It was not easy giving music lessons to eighty kids. The early morning and late evening hours of marching and memorizing music for parades and halftime performances often took its toll on him. The schedules had glitches. There were scary car accidents on the way to music festivals. Surprise requirements placed on the band at contests only added to the unexpected. The football coaches felt anxious for their jobs because they had losing seasons and the band seemed to capture all the positive headlines in the local newspaper. And now Jake was facing an unpredictable situation that could determine his future as a teacher at St. John.

He sat in Don Kitch's office. Boxes of books and memorabilia crowded the room. Don had hired Jake, promising to support his efforts to turn inexperienced teens and preteens into mature students and joyful musicians. They were a team, and Jake did not want to see Don leave. In two weeks he would be in California, and the newly-hired Superintendent would be assuming his duties one month before the new school term.

"Don," asked Jake, "do you know much about your replacement?"

"The announcement of his employment will be made in the newspaper tomorrow, but his name is Emmitt Jennings. He comes from a small community, much like St. John, with a strong football program and less emphasis on music and other school activities. I wasn't sure I should share this information with you, but it's best you know. He was strongly recommended by Coach Morrison, who knew him in another school where they both taught. Does this tell you anything?"

Jake became quiet and thoughtful.

Growing up on the farm, Jake was a healthy eater, never leaving a scrap of food on his plate. Tonight was different. He needed to talk to Katherine—not eat. She listened to him expressing his fears of the unknown.

"I just wonder if this new guy, Emmitt, has any idea how valuable a good music program can be to a school and a community like St. John."

Katherine reached for Jake's hand and squeezed it firmly:

> Classes will begin before long, and then you will know more. Until then, try not to worry too much. You have one more concert in the park a week from Saturday. Just concentrate on bringing happiness to these folks. They love you. They love the band. I know this is hard on you. Having strong backing from a superintendent and

school principal is so necessary to your band program. But, you have always told me, 'If you can fix a problem, then do it and quit worrying. And, if you can't fix it, let it go'. Right now, just stay flexible. Think you can listen to your own good advice?

On hot summer days the band members would set up lemonade stands around the square, selling cool drinks for five cents a glass to bolster their travel funds. On this particular Saturday Coach Morrison invited his friend Emmitt to casually come to St. John for a quiet visit and a drive around town. Approaching the square Hank pointed out the lemonade stands with disgust:

> Emmitt, they have taken over the town. Before Dalke came here we used to be the topic of conversation every Saturday morning. I'd sit in Bobby's Coffee Shop for hours discussing last night's game. Lots of armchair quarterbacks, but at least they were talking football, win or lose. Now it's Jake Dalke this and Jake Dalke that. Know what Oscar Smith told me the other day? He said he and his wife come to the games to see the halftime entertainment by the band. That way if the game is lousy, at least they can still go home feeling like the evening wasn't a waste.

Emmitt looked stern. He and Coach Morrison stopped at one of the local cafés for lunch. They sat in the far corner removed from all the hustle and bustle of noise and shuffling menus. Emmitt leaned in to the coach, looking squarely at his distorted face.

"Hank, before long the boys will be reporting. Are you worried about the upcoming season?" The coach responded quickly.

"Wouldn't you be? I haven't had a winning team for three years. See all these people in here? They've been pretty tolerant, but I don't know how long that can last. This café used to be the hotbed for football talk, but not anymore. There are some very vocal people sitting in here. Some of them wield a lot of influence. And know what? They all seem to love their band and the notoriety it has brought to this town. In fact, there are two guys sitting at that far table who have sons that play in the band and also play for me. I'm afraid some of these people are going to ask me to leave."

Emmitt responds with certainty.

"Hank, I want you to know I will make every effort to keep the band from being the sole focus of this town. I'm not sure what I can do, but I'll do something. You can count on that. What I need from you is to win a few games this season. You want to bring these folks back to your team? Win some games!"

"Sure feels good to have someone in my corner," said the coach. "Kitch didn't offer me any support. I still can't understand why so many big, strapping, healthy boys want to play in that band. I know some of them are out for the team, but it just splits their loyalties. I mean, look what happened to that band in Omaha. They bombed out! The money they earned for that trip, well, we could have used it to replace our uniforms and resod our field."

The Saturday night concert in the park was the last one for the summer. The crowd was overflowing. Cars had arrived two hours early to park facing the grassy area of the town square. The band was at its best, ending the concert with "Stars and Stripes Forever." Jake put his baton down on his stand, bowed and motioned for the band to stand. It had been another stirring concert, hopefully lifting the spirits of the farmers, who had experienced a less than productive crop once again.

Amidst the dwindling noise of the voices and honking horns, Jake heard a familiar voice.

"Before you pack up, I need to talk to you."

Coach Morrison had been standing in the shadows of the appreciative crowd. Jake responded.

"Sure, just a minute." Looking at Jimmy, his student director, he asked, "Would you mind taking my stand to the school? Also, just put this music on my desk. Thanks a lot."

Looking at Hank, Jake suggested they sit on one of the benches.

"I'm glad you came to the concert. What's on your mind?"

"I didn't hear any of the pieces. I was sitting in my house thinking about some things I wanted to say to you, so I just arrived."

Jake stared at Hank, not saying a word. There was a different demeanor about the coach, He didn't seem angry. He seemed scared. He just sat for a few seconds with both elbows on his knees, leaning forward. He pulled back, straightened up and looked directly at Jake.

"As much as I hate to admit it, our football program has lost lots of prominence in the eyes of all these people who were here tonight for the concert. Seems to me *your* ambitious plans for *your* band have, in many ways, divided this community. I'm sure you understand that."

"Wait a minute. You are the one who needs to understand something, Hank. I support all the programs in this high school. I haven't missed a game, in town or out, of your football team. After our halftime shows Katherine and I sit together to watch. We don't leave early. I go to all the recitals and plays, and still never miss . . . "

Hank interrupted abruptly.

"What I care about is my team. I need my players to focus only on football, and not get up early to practice marching or spend evenings practicing their instruments. Many of their families do not have enough money to send their kids to college. They need scholarships—athletic scholarships! I can guarantee you they won't get any offers playing a drum. You are depriving my kids of their future. There are plenty of boys in this school to go around. Just leave my guys alone."

It was difficult to reason with Hank. Jake had been very flexible in allowing some of the football players to play in the band, especially out of season, and on special occasions that didn't conflict with football practices or games. He had not recruited one boy from the team to learn to play an instrument. Each budding musician had stopped by his office during school hours and asked if Mr. Dalke would teach them to play. His motto? *I'll never turn anyone down who wants to play an instrument or be in my band.* He felt Hank's fears were coming out of losing seasons, a new school superintendent who loved athletics and the sarcastic buzz in the coffee shops. Jake thought, *I have been supportive and flexible to make both programs compatible and workable for everyone.*

The bell sounded, and the announcements were blared into each classroom.

"Welcome, students, to another year. May this year, 1939, be the best year ever for all of you. Now let me introduce some of our new teachers. But, before I do, let's welcome our new superintendent and principal of our high school, Mr. Emmitt Jennings, who comes to us from . . . "

## CHAPTER 10

# Praise

*∽ (noticing and genuinely commenting) ∾*

# and Decency

"Well, land's sake!" "Gawley!" "Hal-le-loo-yah!" These expressions, with a pronounced German brogue, would fly out of Jake's mouth with great enthusiasm, whenever he was excited. They were words of praise for making the effort. He knew how easy it was to fasten on the negatives of life and ignore the positives. Living in St. John in the 1930s was a test of survival. It was not unusual for Katherine and Jake to have middle-of-the-night conversations about the helpless feelings that so many of the townsfolk were experiencing:

> Jake, do you really know how many frightened people live in St. John? They are everywhere—on the streets . . . in the restaurants . . . in Uncle Fred's drugstore . . . in the school . . . at the games . . . in the churches. Know why they are so scared? Because they want things to get better, but down deeply inside themselves they don't believe anything will change. I'm so proud of you. We

51

are in this journey together. Just keep praising these kids.
They offer plenty of hope with every note they play.

On a daily basis his band students heard his motivating philosophy: *We can do it . . . we can make music together . . . I'll get you there. Just follow my baton.*

Omaha was a wake-up call for the band, both in concert and marching. And, of course, there was the unexpected and disastrous sight-reading segment of the contest. A new school year was starting. Jake began the rehearsal with the following words:

> Good morning, band. Our fall concert is fast approaching. We have lots to prepare for, including all the halftime routines for the home games. We have also been asked to do a show at one of our away games. Any questions? So, eh, I think you all remember our trip to Omaha. I'm sure you are glad to have that experience behind us. (*Audible groans from the band members*). Regarding the sight-reading part of the competition, well, I take full responsibility for not preparing you properly. You did your best. That is all I asked from you. Thank you, thank you for getting us through that very difficult moment. You are simply a wonderful group of young musicians! Our future together is very bright. Now, one of the main attractions for our fall concert will be a sight-reading demonstration. Since this will again be one of the requirements at the nationals in Colorado Springs, we need to put ourselves to the test. The truth is, band, if we are worth our salt as a musical organization, we will be able to play a piece of music that none of us has seen before and play it as it is written. And I will be much better prepared this time. One more thing. As many of you know when I came here a little over three years ago I requested we have a band mothers club. Many of your moms are part of this group. They have stood behind us from the beginning. If we needed anything done, from raising money for our trips to helping drive to our band festivals . . . well, they have always been willing. We need to recognize how important they have been to each of us. Let's play this concert for them.

## Praise and Decency

Townsfolk have crowded into the high school auditorium for the anticipated fall concert. The curtain opens. The band sits at attention in their spiffy new uniforms. Jake strides to the podium, bows graciously to parents, friends, and the many people who have come to the concert from surrounding communities. Raising his baton, he leads the band in playing a rousing number, "Knights of the Road." A patriotic medley follows. Then Jake speaks:

> You are such a fine audience. Thank you for being so supportive of your band these past few years. I marvel at the progress these kids have made. They have practiced extremely hard and spent long hours learning their marching routines. I know how pleased they are to play for you tonight. But, they are especially honored to play for a special group of women who have stood by our sides since this band was formed. They are the band mothers club. I cannot thank them enough for their financial and emotional support. Thank you . . . thank you.

Jake acknowledges the spontaneous applause and continues:

> One of the elements of the competition at the nationals, but not at the districts, is sight-reading. We had no idea that would be asked of us when we were in Omaha last May. Consequently, we were not prepared. Well, let's say, I was not prepared. These kids certainly did their part to pull me through that anxious time. We do not want that to happen to us again. So, tonight, as part of our concert we are going to attempt to sight-read a number none of us has seen. I have asked my good friend, Benny, the band director at Pratt High School, if he would send to our postmaster some sheets of music that would be unknown to me, so we could practice our sight-reading before you folks here tonight. I asked him to select a difficult number for us. Keep this in mind, neither the band nor I know what is in this envelope.

Jake has captivated the audience. There is a sense that everyone present is not only curious but anticipating what is going to take place. Glenn, the postmaster, comes onto the stage and hands Jake an unopened, large manilla envelope.

The piece is an overture with many difficult passages. Jake looks through the score, marking several complicated passages, writing in bold print the words *soft* and *loud*. Soon his ten minutes are up, and the assigned timer says to Jake and the audience, "It is now time for you to distribute the rest of the music to your band. They will have eight minutes to look at their scores."

Jake roams the stage, handing out music to the section leaders, who in turn give the music to each player. Tonight feels so much different from those anxious moments in Omaha. Jake points out the troublesome passages. There is a buzz in the crowd as many wonder how the band will handle this formidable task.

"Band, notice the repeat on page three and then how the piece moves in and out of softness and loudness on page five. Watch me carefully. I'll do my best to get you through this number. You do your best to hit as many right notes as possible." Jake smiles.

The band does a commendable job, struggling in some passages and playing with confidence in others. Their efforts are rewarded with a loud and enthusiastic response from the audience. Jake bows and, as always, graciously asks the band to stand. Once again he asks the president of the band mothers club to stand.

Indeed, he knows the value of honest praise, and he does not miss the opportunity to bestow it.

## CHAPTER 11

# ETHICS

*(choosing the good)*

# AND DECENCY

Fall morphed into winter, giving the band needed inside time for contest preparations—except for those early morning marching routines and formations on cold brick streets three times a week. Loyal supporters bundled up to watch. The district contests were more critical this year, as only bands receiving highly superior ratings would be allowed to go to Colorado Springs, Colorado for the National Concert and Marching Festival.

Spring welcomed the budding of trees and flowers and a possible trip to the mountains, Jake found his focus and concentration being tested. His reputation for developing a band of musicians with national ranking had spread throughout the Midwest. The St. John News quoted an out-of-town salesman as saying:

"Well, I heard of the St. John band before I heard of St. John."

And the city clerk said, "I, for one, am glad that I know the St. John band and live here."

## Knees Lifted High and Toes Pointed

Jake didn't ask for personal recognition. The attention given him came from hard work, boundless energy, and a belief that music would soothe hurting hearts in the community troubled by hard times.

A letter arrived on his desk, labeled CONFIDENTIAL. It read:

> Dear Mr. Dalke:
> We want to congratulate you on the progress of your band. We have been noticing your talent and want to offer you a job. We have an opening in the band department here at the University of Missouri. We know you may not be able to come immediately, but we are willing to keep the position open for one year to accommodate you. The salary is negotiable. We hope to hear from you.
> Sincerely,
> Professor Robert Smithers,
> Chairman of the Music Department.

Jake closed his office door and pondered the offer. It was certainly an honor to be asked. It would be a major decision in his life and his family's to move from a small town like St. John to the large city of Columbia. There would be no more town square events or moments with car horns honking their appreciation. No more Saturday nights strolling in and out of small local stores, greeting everyone with a familiar first name. No more sense of making a difference in people's lives. He folded the letter and put it in his desk. In two more days he would give them his answer.

The days passed, and the students continued their balancing act between many practices, lessons, homework, and family time. Jake continued to receive invitations for nearby town parades and statewide patriotic events. It was difficult to know whether to accept or decline. One particular letter, however, caught Jake's eye. Upon reading and re-reading the words on embossed stationery, he requested a meeting with Superintendent Jennings to discuss the band's probable acceptance of the invitation.

"Thanks for seeing me. You may know this next year New York City is hosting the World's Fair. Today I received an invitation from the bandmaster of the City Band of New York requesting our band to play at the fair next summer."

Emmitt shakes his head negatively.

"Yes, I know about the World's Fair. Is this the reason you want to talk to me?"

"I just want to visit about the possibility of our band going to New York and participating in this once-in-a-lifetime event. It may not be a good idea, but let me read more of the letter to you."

In his effort to show disinterest Emmitt picks up several papers on his desk, begins shuffling them, walks over to his wall clock, opens the glass, and moves the minute hand to the exact time. Jake reads aloud:

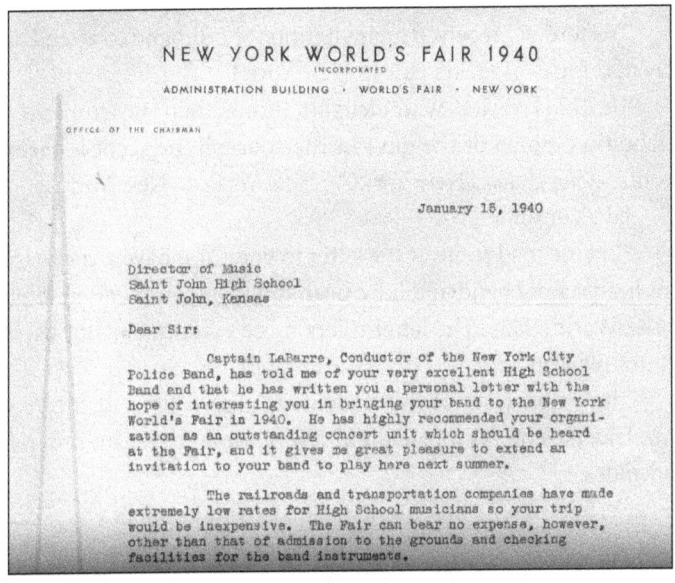

"I have heard much about your band from a relative who used to live in Kansas. She says we would be missing out on something special if we didn't invite you to participate in the 1940 World's Fair here in New York City. It gives me great pleasure to extend an invitation to you and your fine musical organization. I hope we will have the privilege of scheduling your band on our calendar of events. The railroads have made extremely low rates for high school musicians, so your trip would be . . . "

Emmitt interrupts.

"You don't have to read further. The answer is no. I don't care what the reason is or who has invited your band. That's it, no! How could you raise enough money for ninety to a hundred students and chaperones to go to New York? This school needs money for other programs. As far as I'm concerned, you have had your last fundraiser."

The band is seated and ready for their rehearsal. Jake comes out of his office and steps onto the platform. He stares for a few seconds at the music on his stand, then looks up at the band and addresses them.

"Yesterday I received an invitation for our band to attend and play at the 1940 World's Fair in New York City."

The kids shriek with delight, lifting their instruments in celebration. Some of the guys in the sousaphone section begin a spontaneous chant. "New York . . . New York . . . New York."

Jake continues,

"Let me read some of the letter to you. 'You have a very excellent high school band and have been highly recommended to play at the World's Fair.' The letter offers more compliments to us, but I'll not read on."

The enthusiasm of the students is almost too much to contain. Jake taps on his music stand several times to regain order. He continues.

"While I know this would be lots of fun for all of you, I don't want any interruption in our preparation for next year's nationals in Kansas City."

A hush falls over the group. The chants have now turned to silence, and every band member's face is looking attentively toward their conductor.

"I called the bandmaster in New York this morning and told him that while we appreciated the offer, we would not be playing at the World's Fair."

There is continued silence. It is as if time stands still. The past two minutes had been a microcosm of life, full of ecstasy and agony. Jake knows he has made the best decision for his band, the parents and the community. With prayerful thought, he could not have done it any other way.

"I know you are disappointed, but I ask for your trust and belief that this is what is the very best for all of you. Oh, yes, one other announcement. I heard on the radio that a spring snow storm is coming our way later tonight. We still need to practice our marching so wear your galoshes and lots of warm clothes. Eat a good supper and be at the football field at 7:00 o'clock. And, bring your Mentholatum for your noses and throats. I need you to stay healthy. Drink your Bosco!"

The banner stretched over the entrance of the high school building. It read:

## ON TO COLORADO SPRINGS

Was the band ready? Jake had spent many hours preparing for the district contest. The judges had been most helpful in critiquing the band's first place finish, in both concert and marching.

"Pay close attention to your intonation, attacks and releases . . . watch your lines . . . keep them straight . . . raise those knees to the same height, and point those toes."

Jake knew there was always room for improvement and learning. His band was a metaphor for life. Keep putting one foot in front of the other. Celebrate good feelings along the way, but know that each experience, joyful or painful, is another opportunity to gain wisdom in life. He encouraged his students to take a time-out, to reflect on where they were and what they could do to feel better about themselves.

The morning departure arrived. The musicians had learned their lesson from last year's trip to Omaha. This was their moment in the mountain sun. The buses were loaded. It was 6 a.m. Parents, teachers, and other students had climbed out of their warm beds to cheer on the Pride of St. John. By 5 p.m. the buses rolled

## Knees Lifted High and Toes Pointed

into Colorado Springs and the Antlers Hotel, headquarters for the festival.

Three days before the band left, the following telegram arrived at the high school. It was from the coordinator of the contest:

> JJDALKE – ST. JOHN, KANS
> DUE TO UNUSUALLY LARGE REGISTRATION NECESSARY TO RUN SPECIAL EXTRA SESSION OF C AND D BANDS . . . SINCE YOU ARRIVE ON WEDNESDAY YOU ARE SCHEDULED TO PLAY CONCERT AND SIGHTREADING AT 6:30 P.M. THURSDAY. YOUR COMMITTEE FEELS THAT IS A BETTER TIME FOR YOU . . . WILL NOT HAVE AS MUCH TENSION AS ON FRIDAY. YOUR COOPERATION GREATLY APPRECIATED.
> CONFIRM COLLECT.

Jake felt this schedule change was a gift. On Thursday morning the band had a two-hour intensive rehearsal in the hotel's ballroom, with a lighter practice scheduled for the afternoon. Always aware of the energies of his young musicians, he felt the band was ready for their competition. He spoke to them with feeling.

"You sound ready. Now, I want you to relax and enjoy this beautiful place. I know at least thirty-six of you have not been to Colorado. Take a long look at the lingering snow on the majestic peaks. You will never see that in Kansas. We will load the buses after lunch for a jaunt to Cheyenne Mountain and the Garden of the Gods. We should return by five o'clock, in time for you to dress into your uniforms, have a short warm-up and a snack, and then go to the auditorium for our concert playing and sight-reading. Have a fun day. I'm awfully proud of you."

With the spirit of the St. John community present in each one of them, the band members stepped on to the spacious city auditorium stage. There was a huge audience and the ever-imposing judges. Each student sat poised. Their reputation had preceded them as an extraordinary musical organization from a small town. The contest coordinator greeted the large gathering and enthusiastically announced,

## Ethics and Decency

"Welcome to all of you. I am happy to present our next band. Under the direction of professor of music Jake Dalke, here is the St. John, Kansas Tiger Concert Band."

Applause rang throughout the huge, packed auditorium. Jake entered from a side curtain. All year the band had waited for this moment. He raised his baton. Their instruments became braced against their mouths. As they struck the first chord of "March Blue Bells," the sound was overpowering, even to Jake. This group could play! It was an electric moment. Their second number was the required piece, *Overture Militaire*, and they finished with "Dublin Holiday."

By the overwhelmingly loud applause, it seemed the band did beautifully. But Jake knew judges had certain idiosyncrasies. It would take only one or two low critiques to keep them from the win of a lifetime. The results wouldn't be known until morning.

Telegrams kept pouring in:

> DEAR MR. DALKE AND BAND – BEST WISHES FOR TWO FIRSTS BEST OF LUCK WAITING FOR YOU TO BRING HOME THE BACON

Curfew was 10 p.m., with the request that all band members be ready to practice their marching routines by 9:30 the next morning. Demonstrations would be presented to the judges in the afternoon. Of course, in the back of everyone's mind was the result of their concert presentation. It was difficult to wait for the judges' decision. The kids had worked so hard, poring over every possible dynamic in the musical scores to enhance the sound and present what the composer had intended. Tomorrow couldn't come fast enough.

Will Roger's Stadium was the marching venue. There wasn't an empty seat. The band stood at attention while the announcer made the stirring introduction. Drum major Bill King blew three crisp sounds from his whistle, and the routine began, knees lifted high and toes pointed. The band didn't miss one step or yard line. As one observer said, "If there is such a thing as perfection, we just witnessed it."

# Knees Lifted High and Toes Pointed

Soon after the marching competition was finished, the results were posted, along with the concert and sight-reading results from the day before. As Jake anxiously scanned them, he let out a loud, "Hal-le-loo-yah. We did it! Katie, look here . . . we did it . . . we are national champions!"

Band members, who had gathered around the bulletin board, began to cheer and cry. Many scrambled to find pay phones and call their parents. Jake immediately notified Western Union and sent the following telegram back home:

> COLO SPRINGS COLO 9:49 P.M. MAY 12
> JUST RECEIVED RATINGS NATIONAL CHAMPIONS IN CONCERT AND SIGHT-READING MORE TO FOLLOW. JJ DALKE

And, then, a second telegram, one hour later:

> COLO SPRINGS COLO 10:49 P.M. MAY 12
> MARCHING NATIONAL CHAMPIONS WILL ARRIVE BETWEEN SIX AND TEN JJ DALKE

An attached note from one judge summed up the feelings of the other six with the words, "This is good band work of which your community can well be proud."

A special edition of the newspaper was published honoring the National Champions. They were to arrive Saturday, a day the paper is not normally published. In fact, in the special edition, the editor said:

> Congratulations Band! Several months ago we discontinued our Saturday paper, but when the good news concerning the band arrived, we felt the most we could do for them was none too much. Therefore, we resolved to publish a 'band extra' carrying a good account of the numerous activities of our grand organization, and also all the congratulatory cards we could procure. We worked hard and fast all morning to get this edition out, and present it to our readers in honor of the band. So, this publication of the 'Band Issue' shows how proud of you we are and offers our heartiest CONGRATULATIONS.

## Ethics and Decency

An additional article summarized the band's success with the words:

> Five years ago St. John High School did not have a band. There was little interest along musical lines. Slowly, but with tenacity, Jake Dalke began inviting students to try an instrument. 'See if you like it,' he would say. Then the folks around town began to notice some semblance of a band organization. A citizen or two gave a dollar to support a band fund, buy uniforms, upgrade instruments, or volunteer to drive to festivals. Something also began to happen in the lives of a few novice musicians. They liked to play. They practiced and encouraged their friends to join the band. It was fun. There was a new sound in town. Contests were entered, second and third places were garnered. Then, the band began to think like a championship band. Their attitude changed from 'We are just OK' to 'We are something special.' That was five years ago.

Amid the beeping of horns, cheers and whistles, the band rolled into town at 10:20 p.m. The buses were met thirty-five miles west of St. John by a large number of cars, which escorted the ecstatic musicians into town, honking all the way. Celebrations went into the night, especially in the homes of the band members. The next day preachers spoke of the band in their sermons. It seemed St. John had been reborn.

A valued letter of congratulations from former school superintendent, Don Kitch, was quite welcomed. It was in deep contrast to what was on the horizon. Ever since the band developed into a viable and important organization in the school system and community, there were some undertones and rumblings concerning the attention the band was receiving over the athletic programs, namely football. Jake recalled an earlier, brief encounter with Hank, the football coach. Now, once again, the tension was growing as the band grabbed the headlines in the newspapers, and the townsfolk referred to them as the Pride of St. John. Some students and parents wanted athletics to be the center of everyone's interest. Once again Jake found himself in Superintendent Jennings' office.

# CHAPTER 12

# LEADERSHIP

*ও (encouraging the vision) ৬ও*

# AND DECENCY

"School's out... school's out... the teachers let the..." Well, almost. Two weeks remained until the spring term ended. It was usually a non-productive time for students and teachers. There were last minute make-up tests, class hikes around town, and sack lunches on the grass inside the town square. The band members were turning in some of their music and talking through what pieces to keep for summer concerts in the park and neighboring parades. Jake was sorting a multitude of musical scores, tapping out some of the rhythms with his baton while making audible voice sounds. He could hear every instrument playing the score flawlessly inside his head. A soft knock on the half-opened band room door jarred him from his musical fantasies. It was Emmitt's secretary. Rather apologetically she said,

"Mr. Dalke. I'm sorry to bother you. Superintendent Jennings would like to see you in his office as soon as possible." Her demeanor was compassionate, offering a silent clue for Jake to be on his guard.

"Sure, tell him I'll be there in ten minutes, when class is over."

As Jake approached Emmitt's office, he remembered the last time his ideas were rudely dismissed. He wasn't looking forward to another encounter with this uncompromising, powerful man. He thought, *He came into this job not liking me, and I haven't been able to change his mind.* Jake knocked on the closed door. With a voice two octaves lower than usual, Emmitt said, "Come in. Have a seat."

He stayed behind his huge desk, swiveling back and forth in a cushioned chair, often with his back to Jake. In a determined motion like a prize fighter winding up for the final blow to the opponent's body, he rotated his chair towards Jake and unceremoniously announced,

"It's time for some things to change. As you know, we had another mediocre football season, and although Coach Morrison has not talked to me about it, I know he feels very badly. In fact, some of the boosters are wondering if he should move on. Quite frankly, Jake, he won't leave here as long as I'm the superintendent and principal of this high school."

He rises from his chair to make his next point, planting his index finger against his chest with poorly-disguised hostility

"I know, as well as you, that the band gets all the publicity. The newspaper calls them the Pride of St. John. It's as though athletics rate the second page of the paper, and you get all the headlines. Something has got to change. I have watched this year with great interest, and I believe you should consider moving on."

Emmitt gestured to the door, but Jake did not budge. The gauntlet that had been thrown down a few years ago was now being picked up. Jake spoke firmly:

> I know your interest in this high school is football first, basketball second and the music department third, if even that. I want you to know two things: I'm not leaving, at least on my own. And, secondly, I will not compromise our music program because a few parents blame the poor record of the football team on the band. That's ridiculous,

and I believe you know it. Boys and girls need music. Not everyone is a talented athlete. Some of them don't even care about sports. But they like music, and they need what I can offer them.

Unmoved, Emmitt leans across his desk, and says bluntly, "I can see you aren't going to take my advice. You have sealed your fate. This is a matter for the school board."

The minute Jake left Emmitt's office the word spread about an urgently-called school board meeting the next evening. Throughout the town rumors began to fly like the seasonal dust storms. Telephone lines were busy, and people stopped one another on the street to speculate about the demise of the music program.

The board members were all notified about Emmitt's request for the emergency meeting. Jake kept picturing the board members. He felt their support. He also knew a couple of them were frustrated with the athletic program. Interestingly, the board had not changed since Jake was hired five years ago.

The time had come. Jake and Emmitt sat at opposite ends of the large table. Walter called the meeting to order.

"This emergency gathering of the St. John School Board will now come to order. Our school superintendent, Emmitt Jennings, has requested our presence tonight. It is my understanding you have some concerns about Jake's band, Emmitt. Is this right?"

They were a casually-dressed group in their overalls and flannel shirts, wearing caps advertising implement and fertilizer companies. Their faces had late spring farmer's tans, with Harold, the banker, being the exception. Pads of paper and pencils had been carefully placed in front of each board member. They were more than ready to hear what Emmitt had to say.

"Thank you, Walter. Yes, that's right. I do have some concerns as your superintendent and high school principal, but I'm not the only one. There are many parents and other people in this town who believe our athletic programs are suffering because of Jake's influence on the kids in our school. It seems like more kids would rather play in his band than put on a football or basketball uniform."

Butch seeks clarification.

"Emmitt, how many parents and, well, other adults would you guess are upset?"

"Let me think. I'd guess there are a number of them. I don't know exactly, but I hear complaints, especially during football season. Some people in our town go to the football games to see the halftime show, not the game. What kind of support is that to kids who are busting their butts to have a winning season?"

Butch continues, "So, would it be fair to say, only a few parents are concerned, and that could be because they aren't winning football games like they used to several years ago? I mean, are you really getting as many complaints as it sounds?"

Emmitt begins to squirm as Butch looks straight into his eyes.

"You know what, Emmitt? I don't hear too much on the streets, except for a few diehard disgruntled old codgers who sit in the café and drink coffee on Saturday morning and replay every run, pass, and kick from the night before. But let me tell you another thing. I see those same old codgers at the band concerts. Before my son Alan graduated, he was able to do both, play in the band and do football, and he excelled at both. Emmitt, I just wonder where all the pressure you are feeling is really coming from?"

Emmett replies,

"Butch, I thought you were a strong supporter for athletics here in St. John, but, well, I can see your wife has gotten to you." He laughs but is the only one doing so.

Walter speaks, "Anything else, Emmitt?"

"Yes. There is one more thing that ought to interest all of you. I talked to Elton, our board attorney, and he told me our school will have less funds available for the next year, which means we will need to distribute our money more carefully. As your superintendent I keep a careful eye on the school budget. I know the music department gets more than its share of funds, so that will be a place to begin cutting."

Again, Walter asks, "What else is on your mind?"

"That's all. Just take it seriously."

Walter looks at Jake. "Do you have anything you would like to say?"

Jake stands from his chair and confidently looks at the six members of the board, purposely avoiding eye contact with Emmitt:

> I came here five years ago. I sat in this very room and heard you gentlemen say there was only one student in this town who could play an instrument. You basically painted a hopeless picture for the music department. Today there are one hundred kids who play instruments, and they play very well. This band has brought hope, pleasure, and new life to this town. I've made some mistakes. I've paced the floor in the middle of the night wondering what I could do differently to bring about harmony in this school and town. I know I've gotten mixed up at times, and felt this band was mine, when it really belongs to each of you, this community, and the kids. Katherine has helped me to see what true leadership is. It is to inspire others to be curious with their minds and confident in their abilities. I may have helped to create the desire that is tucked away in these kids, but they have created the music. That's it, gentlemen. I don't have anything else to say.

"Thank you, Jake." Walter continues. "Both of you can step outside in the hallway. We need to discuss a few things, and then we'll call you back in."

The hall felt empty of noise and devoid of energy. Jake hadn't realized how walls and floors come alive with the sounds of lockers banging, kids shouting and feet creating their own uneven beat. For years he had been marching down the streets to the sounds of human decency. Now he felt nothing but uneasy silence. The two men stood across from one another, shifting from one foot to the other, and pretending to be interested in the most miniscule cracks in the wall. The awkward tension was momentarily interrupted as Emmett said,

"Jake, you better be prepared for what you're going to hear when we go back in."

## Leadership and Decency

Walter opened the door of the boardroom and invited both men to return to the table. "Please sit down."

There is a dramatic pause as Walter looks down at his notes, then straight at Emmitt.

"Emmitt, we are asking for your resignation by the middle of the summer. We also expect you to honor your contract these remaining two months. Jake, good luck as you move through the summer and prepare for your next national contest in Kansas City."

After hearing what happened to Emmitt, Hank decided to resign, giving the board time to interview through the summer for another football coach.

Jake's leadership was never questioned. It was embraced. Under his careful and thoughtful guidance, the band continued to grow in numbers, enthusiasm and skill. There was no word on the street about why two key resignations occurred so abruptly. No one needed to talk about the board's decision. Townsfolk knew the answer.

## CHAPTER 13

# Continual Fine-Tuning
*(commitment to excellence)*
# and Decency

JUNE ARRIVED AND BAND members fell into more predictable routines. School was over and it was time to begin the summer concerts, plus one more contest. The band had accepted an invitation to compete in the state contest, sponsored by the Veterans of Foreign Wars. The playing and marching competition would be held at the fair grounds in Hutchinson. Fresh from their national victory in Colorado Springs, St. John entered this contest with great confidence. Jake felt this festival would continue to keep the band sharp in their marching and well-tuned in their instrumentation.

The band repeated the same performance they offered at the nationals. They were in a class all by themselves. Their precise marching and brilliantly played overture gave the band first place by more than nine points. The Hutchinson newspaper praised all the bands, and especially St. John's, with the following editorial:

> It was a fine sight, those bands marching across the field maneuvering intricately and playing with musical

## Continual Fine-Tuning and Decency

precision those martial airs which set your feet to moving and run shivers up your spine. The VFW is to be thanked for bringing to Hutchinson again for a grand summer's night concert the bands which we only have a chance to hear during the hubbub of fair-time. Behind the music, the marching, and the gay uniforms are hours of labor and boundless enthusiasm. St. John's band, national high school champion and winner here, is the result of training which started long before anyone thought of entering a contest. St. John should be tremendously proud of its young musicians, as should be the neighboring towns. Yet the point to this labor, so briefly rewarded, is that it is prompted by a real appreciation of music, the most civilizing of arts. We in Kansas have that appreciation. Back east, in the cities, many believe only dust flourishes on the wide prairie. Let them hear our bands. We have culture because we have worked for it. We may enjoy such stirring music not because some rich man endowed an orchestra, but because the neighbor boy wanted to play the clarinet and sister yearned for a bassoon and because the entire community encouraged them with good teaching in the schools. School bands make the real music of democracy.

With the success the band had enjoyed during the past school year—and now another victory in the VFW festival—Jake wanted to keep his young musicians sharp, have some fun together and play a few Saturday night concerts in the park. What does one do to top being a national champion? Jake knew the answer—give them a new stimulating experience that would keep them from growing complacent. Go to camp Carlile for a five-day band camp. What a wonderful idea.

Camp Carlile was less than twenty miles from St. John. Seventy-eight band members—those who were not helping in harvest—chose to attend. The band mothers, ever loyal to Jake since his arrival in St. John five years ago, offered to arrange all the meals, secure chaperones, and be present throughout the five days to tend to any concerns or needs.

## KNEES LIFTED HIGH AND TOES POINTED

A few band directors from the area gladly accepted Jake's invitation to be sectional rehearsal teachers. The big attraction, however, was Professor Russell Wiley, the band director at the University of Kansas, who agreed to stay the full five days and serve as an instructor and guest conductor.

On the staff of the high school was a young man named Bill Martin Jr, the drama and speech teacher, who later became famous with his writings for children and elementary school teachers, such as *Brown Bear, Brown Bear, What Do You See?* Bill served as the recreational director for the camp.

Each day began at 7 a.m. with breakfast, followed by a full band rehearsal. The morning culminated with the learning of marching routines for the up-and-coming football halftime performances and parades. The afternoons were for relaxation and recreation, plus one hour of sectional rehearsals. Before bedtime everyone gathered around the campfire for singing and storytelling. Charlie, first chair in the trumpet section, played taps each evening as lights faded into the quietness of the revered surroundings.

## Continual Fine-Tuning and Decency

On the last evening of the camp, Jake invited everyone in the county to a concert at the site. As he stated to the many attendees:

> I feel that the camp has been very successful. New members have become adjusted to the type of music that is played in the advanced band. The work accomplished at the camp has been equivalent to approximately six weeks of school work. However, this project could not have been successful or served its purpose, had it not been for the wholehearted cooperation of the band mothers club. The students received good training in music, wonderful food and wholesome recreation, led by our own Bill Martin. And, last but certainly not least, I want to thank all the guest band directors who have assisted in our breakout sessions. Particularly I want to recognize my friend, Professor Russell Wiley, from Kansas University, who has given so generously of his time this week. I thank all of you for coming tonight. And now, it is time for you to hear your students play. We are happy you are here.

Darkness had set in. Jake began directing. In the middle of the Sousa march there was a loud pop and the camp grounds were immersed in a blackout—no lights anywhere. Murmurs rumbled through the crowd until everyone realized that the band was continuing to play by memory. The students were used to playing most of their numbers without music except for complicated overtures. Quickly some of the camp personnel rounded up a few lanterns and hung them strategically near the audience and band members.

The concert continued with the playing of *The Traveler Overture*, a large orchestral piece with several main sections, purposefully performed undirected. The "Star Spangled Banner" ended the evening. Everyone departed for home, refreshed and amazed.

## CHAPTER 14

# MORE THAN MELODY
### *(the blessing of music to a community)*
# AND DECENCY

SPRING IS A WONDERFUL time of year in St. John. The leaves create a shelter from the soft rains. The sun brings out rainbows. Birds have returned home and are chirping in melodious pronouncements. The town square is alive with people who have hibernated through the harsh winter and are now emerging to visit with one another on Saturday evenings. Farmers are anticipating and praying for healthy crops. And, ol' Frank heads for the café. The seasons may change, but Frank never does. He wears his same khakis and WWI cap.

## More Than Melody and Decency

The summer hurries by, and the school doors swing open for another year. The football halftime performances are more difficult and entertaining, with patriotism being the main theme. Because of World War II, these presentations could not be diluted in the least. Such a theme would hit the hearts of many people who had young men in the war. Jake spent many hours designing the marching routines and selecting the appropriate music. His twirlers dressed as Uncle Sam. The band played "The Sidewalks of New York", "K-K-Katy", "It's a Long Way to Tipperary", "God Bless America", and "Anchors Aweigh." At one of the halftime shows the band two-stepped to the tune of "Alexander's Ragtime Band." Each performance ended with "God Bless America." The programs demanded much from the band. Not only did they have to concentrate on their marching while performing from memory, but they were being asked to play tunes so familiar to the audience that they needed to present them as perfectly as possible.

The annual Christmas program was played to a standing-room only crowd. Jake included on the program the requested number for the national competition. Was he thinking next spring at this winter concert? The band knew, as they played that particular number on that cold December evening, that it was not the last time they would see that piece of music. They would eat and sleep every measure and every nuance found in the composer's heart. There was no doubt—the band was going to be ready—or would they?

It seems everything was falling into place for a possible third straight national contest win, and this time in Kansas City, Missouri. Except for one thing. The band was displaying unusual disinterest and lethargy. Had the students grown too accustomed to winning? Had the demanding fall schedule of performances taken its toll? Several musicians kept missing notes and entrances. There was a lack of concentration.

"Come on, band," pleads Jake. "You're just not cutting it this morning. Let's try again."

The band begins to repeat the number, only to have Jake stop them in the middle of it.

"I need your attention. Trumpets, you come in on the second beat, not the third, and clarinets, I need sharper, crisper notes from you at measure thirty. Kansas City will be here before we know it. Now, play like you mean it."

As he directs, he keeps asking himself, *What is wrong with these kids? Have they lost their desire? Maybe they have become too cocky. Have I worn them out?* He stops them again, lays down his baton, and with disappointment says,

"Pass in your music . . . all of it. You aren't working nearly hard enough. We have three weeks till districts, and you aren't close to being ready. At this rate we won't even qualify for the nationals. You are dismissed."

Jake goes to his office and wonders if he should have accepted that position at the University of Missouri? *Have I worn out my welcome here in this little town?*

Bill and Jimmy, his student directors, tap lightly on the door.

"May we come in?" asks Bill.

"Sure. Want to sit down?"

The boys remain standing in front of Jake's desk. Jimmy speaks.

"We want to apologize for what happened just now. Maybe we are tired, or something, but, well . . . "

Bill intercedes. "We want you to give us the music."

Jake is surprised. "Why?"

"Please, Mr. Dalke. Just give us the contest numbers . . . all the music for each section. We will bring it back by tonight's practice."

Not sure what to make of the request, Jake reluctantly hands them a stack of music. The boys dash down the hallways, finding the various section leaders.

"Hey Tony, take this music and give it to everyone in your section. Tell them to practice every chance they can before tonight's rehearsal. Then bring it all back to us by 6:45 so we can turn it in to Mr. Dalke."

The same message was enthusiastically delivered to every section leader. Musical sounds could be heard all over the town as kids practiced during study halls, at home and on park benches. That evening Jake experienced the best rehearsal of the year. Confidence spilled over like the rushing waters of Niagara Falls. The band evolved that day with a new sense of commitment and passion for themselves, their director and their community.

A week later, after reaching their fundraising goals for their trip to Kansas City, an Appreciation Concert was held in the school auditorium. It was Katherine's idea. The purpose was to recognize all the assistance the band had received from community organizations, friends, boosters, and parents to make the Kansas City trip possible. Besides, it would be a great tune-up before heading to the district contest and then the nationals.

Thank you notes were to be given to all in attendance. She presented her idea to the newspaper for assistance in printing. The publisher stood across the counter from her, figuring how much the notes would cost. Finally, he said, "Based on four hundred notes done on heavy, off-white colored paper, here is the price." He handed her a paper that read:

"Congratulations to the Pride of St. John. We will be happy to print your announcements at no cost."

## Knees Lifted High and Toes Pointed

The concert was a tremendous success, but it was more than music. It was a stirring moment never experienced by any person in this little town. All required selections for the national band festival were on the program, including the clarinet quartet, brass sextet, twirlers and pianists. The band played their contest numbers, allowing the audience to hear what they would be presenting in Kansas City. Jake often ended the band's performances with Sousa's "Stars and Stripes Forever." Today's rendition had a different touch. As the familiar themes of the famous composition were presented, different sections stood to perform their highlighted musical passages. The piccolo solo was precise and without hesitation. The grand finale featured the brass section forming a line across the stage, playing each note with the precision of a metronome.

Jake waited on the edge of the stage, continuing to acknowledge his band and their most magnificent concert. He couldn't help but notice a lone figure standing in the front row. Leading the applause, with clapping hands outstretched over his WWI-capped head, was Frank.

# CHAPTER 15

# Shared Healing

*ↄ (putting sounds on a dream) ↄ*

# and Decency

THE PORCH SWING WAS a mellow place to think, meditate, and talk. Katherine broke the silence. "Tomorrow we leave for Kansas City. You seem pretty relaxed." Jake responded, rather pensively.

"I was sitting in the band room today after practice, watching those kids leave, one by one. All the memories of six years ago flashed in front of me. When we came here this town was like a barren piece of land. Crop failures symbolized the spirit of the people. I think of what I had to work with and the hours and hours of lessons. My lands! If I had a penny for every hour I've spent with these kids, we'd be as wealthy as Henry Ford! So, I just sat there on that old rickety stool and realized it has all been worth it. Katherine, I've done all I can do. It's up to each of them now."

Katherine hands Jake a letter that arrived earlier that day. It was from Don Kitch.

"Here, I thought you should read this before going to bed. It might be just the medicine you need for a peaceful night's rest." Jake opens the letter and begins reading:

> Dear Jake and Katie, it's been quite a while since we have spoken or corresponded. I have thought of both of you so much and can honestly say there are many moments I wish I were back in St. John, working and playing. This job is quite different, with lots of pressures. Guess it all goes with the territory. What I'm really writing about is to offer my heartiest congratulations to you and the band members on their wonderful achievements. Your reputation is quite well known, even here in California. In fact, one of the teachers cornered me the other day and asked what it would take to get you here as our music instructor. I still take the St. John News, and it gives me a thrill to read, almost on a daily basis, how well the band is doing. It seems like such a short time ago that we were just trying to round up old instruments and encourage kids to try to play. But that was then. Now you both are headed to Kansas City. I wish you great success in the nationals. Give the band my best and pass my respect along to any of my friends you might see.
>
> Sincerely,
> Don

## Shared Healing and Decency

Last time the band played at the old train station, it had been for a group of young soldiers going off to boot camp. The old elongated red brick building has a bold black-and-white sign which reads **St. John, Kansas**. It is a landmark in the town. It is where the agony of tears and the ecstasy of smiles happen at least three times a day. Suitcases and instruments are now placed on the splintered loading carts held up by oversized rusty iron wheels. Kids are holding their neatly-pressed uniforms in garment bags as they make a last check on all their belongings.

"Mom, did you pack my sweater?"

"I can't find my music. Hope I didn't leave it on the kitchen table."

"Wonder where I put my puzzle book?"

The porter has lived in St. John for many years and is a fixture at the station. Elijah and his wife are one of the three black families in the town. He is gray around the temples and quite bald, although most patrons don't notice since he rarely removes his porter's cap. His physique is deceptively frail, as he has loaded and unloaded heavy suitcases for years. When the Armstrongs moved to St. John they bought a house next door to Elijah and Helen. He begins to assist many of the students with their belongings and smaller instruments. That he loves his work is evidenced by his kindness and attentiveness.

"Here, let me take that. That's almost as big as you are."

"My, my, you kids are going to have a wonderful time in the big city."

"Oh yes, I believe you kids are going to win again."

"Sure hope you enjoy your train ride."

Steam rises from beneath the train's engine, wrapping around huge wheels. Smoke billows from the smokestack, making animal shapes that tantalize one's fantasy. Every other minute a loud sound blasts from the train's whistle reminding folks for miles around how fortunate they are to have such transportation in their little town. Kids keep chatting with their parents until they hear,

"All aboard! All aboard for Kansas City."

## Knees Lifted High and Toes Pointed

As the train rumbles down the track, Jake begins thinking out loud about the contest. "Wonder what piece the judges will select for us to sight-read?"

Katherine looks at Jake for a few seconds before responding. "I don't know, but I'll bet you will get your kids through it."

Jake's mind flashes back to the band's last trip to Kansas City for the American Royal, and the detestable encounter in the hotel dining room. " . . . *The coloreds can't sit here. They will have to sit in their own section, at the back.*" Those words still sicken him.

He pictures Katherine, Cleo and Charlene walking to the rear of the dining room to sit alone, while he sits, helplessly demoralized, with the rest of the band. *Those kids did not deserve that kind of inhumane treatment, and they certainly don't deserve it now.*

The train ambles into Central Station, where a city bus is waiting to transport the band to the Masonic Temple in downtown Kansas City. This will be their practice location for the next three days. Later, seated in a large room, the kids begin removing their instruments from their cases.

"Okay, band, let's hear how you sound after a long train ride."

They begin the tuning process, all hitting the same note, holding it out, and then with the upward motion of Jake's hand, moving a step higher on the scale. The sound reverberates throughout the temple. Jake speaks:

> Tonight we march at the stadium in front of a huge crowd and eight judges. I have read who the judges are, and I know some of them personally. Others I know by their reputations. They are from the surrounding universities and will be hard to please. They will study our lines and steps more critically than any group of judges we have experienced. They will listen for how well tuned we are, how precisely we attack and release our notes and how we express our feelings in the music and in our marching. I know this competition will be very tough.

Jake pauses. "I . . . I . . . well, I believe in each of you kids. Don't you ever forget that. Tonight let's march with precision and discover the music that is down deep inside each of you."

## Shared Healing and Decency

The announcer's voice sounds throughout the stadium.

"The next band in our competition is from St. John, Kansas. They are under the direction of Jake Dalke. Please welcome the St. John, Kansas Tiger Marching Band."

Bill blows a long shrill sound from his whistle, followed by four crisp bursts. Raising his baton, he brings the band onto the field with a dramatic cadence while it plays a variation of the "Star Spangled Banner"—of course, all by memory. Several folks in the crowd stand and begin to applaud, bringing the rest of the spectators to their feet. Immediately the band breaks into an extremely complex marching routine, weaving in and out of each other's lines. This choreography is accompanied by the "Stars and Stripes Forever" with a brief pause for the piccolo solo. The crowd claps exuberantly as the band exits beneath the goal posts. Bill sighs to himself, *one down, two to go.*

This year the judging is without delay. All the bands re-enter the field and stand at attention to hear the results of the evening's marching competition. "In third place, George Washington High School, from Willow Springs, Oklahoma.

In second place, Fairfield High School, from Canton, South Dakota." A football field full of musicians await the final announcement. The stadium lights bounce in an uncanny rhythm off the bells of the tubas, silently playing their own tune. "*Wear those galoshes . . . don't forget your mentholatum . . . drink your Bosco.*" The players quietly fidget.

"May I have your attention! This year's national champion in the marching competition—the Tiger Marching Band from St. John, Kansas."

The large crowd rises to its feet to pay tribute to the big band from a little town in Kansas.

The band gathers in the corner of the hotel lobby. Jake speaks.

"I know you are overjoyed with tonight's results, but, well, I want you to go upstairs to your rooms, get into some comfortable clothes, hang up your uniforms, and meet me in the ballroom in fifteen minutes."

## Knees Lifted High and Toes Pointed

Many kids sprawl on the hardwood floors. Jake closes the large doors. He does not speak for several seconds.

"Tonight's marching performance was the finest I've ever witnessed. Your knees were high and your toes pointed. You owned the field tonight. You played without error. Congratulations. You warmed the hearts of many people." Jake hesitates.

"Tomorrow some of you will play your last concert numbers and sight-read your last piece of music as a member of this band." He pauses, lifting his glasses to rub his eyes. Band members are heard sniffling. In a quivering voice he continues. "We would not be in this place without your senior leadership. You have been the backbone of our band, and I want to wish you continued strength and (Jake pauses) . . . sorry, I will just miss all of you terribly."

The telegram is wired back home through Western Union:

> MAY 12 BAND WON FIRST IN MARCHING TONIGHT. ALL'S WELL. CONCERT AND SIGHT-READING TOMORROW. JJ DALKE

The concert hall is crowded. The judges arrive, shaking hands with one another and gathering at their table in front of the stage. At the same time, back in St. John, parents, grandparents, and other excited townsfolk are sitting in their kitchens and living rooms glued to their upright Philco radios. Morning shoppers have stopped outside Butch's Appliance store to listen to his radio, which is blaring into the street. The concert and sight-reading portions of the national competition are being broadcast for the first time on nationwide radio.

South of town, Calvin and Velma Armstrong have invited a family from the Methodist Church to listen to the broadcast with them.

"Thank you for joining us," says Calvin. "Our girls have so enjoyed being in the band with your son Joe and the other children. We can't thank Mr. and Mrs. Dalke enough."

Velma goes to the stove for the pot of coffee and refills everyone's cup. Looking at his pocket watch, Calvin urges everyone to gather in the living room, as it is time for the competition to begin.

## Shared Healing and Decency

Moving his antenna towards the window, he finds the broadcast and turns up the volume. "There now, we're set. Come on kids, give it all you've got."

> Welcome to the beautiful concert hall in downtown Kansas City, Missouri. We are at the site of the national high school marching and concert competition. This is station WDAF, 103 on your dial. This is truly a big moment in the lives of these young musicians from all over the country. But it is especially rewarding for a group of one hundred young people from St. John, Kansas. They will be the first band to perform their concert numbers, followed by the sight-reading segment. As many of you in our listening audience know, sight-reading is the measure of a band's true musicianship.

The announcer continues.

> By now many of you are familiar with the story of the music teacher who came to that small town, where there was no music program, no instruments and only one young lady with her grandpa's saxophone, which she could barely play. Today they are called The Pride of St. John. Here is the contest coordinator. Keep those dials set, and let's give a listen.

"Good morning and welcome to the concert and sight-reading portion of our national band competition. Our first band to perform this morning is from St. John, Kansas. They are under the capable direction of Professor of Music, Jake Dalke. Let's hear it for the St. John Kansas Tiger Band!"

With confidence and skill Jake masterfully leads the band in an impressive Sousa march. The second number is the *Eroica Overture*, by Beethoven. They play flawlessly and are well rewarded by shouts and intense clapping. Silently Bill mouths to himself, *whew, two down, one to go.* The contest coordinator speaks again.

"We will give the band a few minutes to rest before entering into the most difficult phase of the competition, the sight-reading." The students stretch, take some deep breaths, and collectively sit down, propping their instruments on their laps.

"Mr. Dalke, are you ready to receive your piece of music? If so, Professor Wiley, our chairman of the judges, will give you the score. Remember, you have ten minutes to study the piece, before talking to your band. Ladies and gentlemen, the piece that has been selected for the St. John Band is an overture titled "The Hero" or *The Hero Overture*. There is an unusual murmur in the crowd. Several people shake their heads, indicating the difficulty of such a number. One band director in the audience is overheard saying,

"This will be very tough. I know some university bands that have trouble with this piece."

The announcer continues.

"Mr. Dalke, copies of the Overture will now be handed to your band. You have eight minutes to visit with them."

The audience grows very quiet, hoping to hear what Jake will say about this difficult piece.

"Band, take out your pencils. Listen very carefully to me. At measure ten there is a key change. Circle it. On page two, measure twenty-eight, circle the pianissimo and then draw a line with an arrow at measure thirty-one and circle the forte. Notice the staccato notes for all brass in measure forty-seven and forty-eight. We hit the first chord with a double forte, rest two counts, and then swell the next chord until I cut you off. Any questions?"

The band members place their pencils inside their music cases. Jake steps off the platform and moves to the middle of the band:

> Put your instruments in your laps. I want to tell you a story. Listen very carefully. This overture is about two lovers. The music has many moods that need precise interpretation to allow the story of these lovers to speak to us. They live on opposite shores. At night, a young man, named Leander, braves the dangerous waters with the guidance of a distant torch on the opposite shore, swimming the strait to be with Hero, his beloved. Night after night Leander makes the long swim, a testimony of his love for Hero. One night, while he is swimming to be with her, a fearful storm arises, lashing at the sea and causing the waters to rage. Leander desperately fights to survive, but his strength fails him, and he drowns. Later

## Shared Healing and Decency

the waves wash him to the shore where Hero finds his lifeless body. In her grief and despair, she throws herself into the water and joins her lover in death. (Jake pauses.) I want you to feel what they must have felt for one another—first joy, then sadness, and then tragedy. Watch me. I'll get you through it. It will be up to you to create the story through your music.

When the last chord was played, there was a moment of silence, much like an amen. Then, with a thunderous roar as if from the heavens, the audience rose to its feet. One by one, the judges stood and applauded. The radio commentor was so choked up he couldn't speak for a few seconds, causing most of the townsfolk back home to jiggle their dials for fear of having lost the broadcast. It was a special moment for the band from St. John. They brought life to their musical dreams. Bill thought, *three down, none to go!*

Results would be announced early afternoon. It was time for a well-deserved early lunch. Entering the hotel restaurant, the band is greeted by the hostess, who begins sizing up the various groups for the available tables. Suspended from her menu table is a sign that reads "Whites Only." Jake, Katherine, Cleo, Charlene, and Bill walk towards the hostess. Jake speaks.

"Where would you like for us to sit?" Caught speechless and fumbling with the menus, she timidly points to the sign. Jake speaks once again,

"Yes, I noticed your sign. Tell me, where would you like for us to sit? Looks like there is a table over there by the window."

Searching for words but trying to be direct, the hostess says,

"Sir, I'm not allowed to seat colored in this restaurant. Down the street there is a little café for coloreds only. You better go there."

Refusing to get caught up in the emotional turbulence, Jake continues,

"Ma'am, I want to introduce you to my wife and Bill and now to Cleo and Charlene. They are two of the finest young ladies I know. They are in my band. We all play music together, travel to parades together, and laugh together, and we also eat together.

There is no difference in our hunger. Now, where would you like for us to sit?"

After dining at the hotel restaurant they quickly walked to the lobby where the contest results were posted on a huge bulletin board. The results were in. Jake hurried to read the announcements. Posted were the words, "First in the nation in concert—St. John Tiger Band from St. John, Kansas." Jake kept searching for the sight-reading scores. The courier pushed her way through the politely impatient kids to post the results. On the scoreboard was a sealed manilla folder addressed to the St. John band. Jake handed the envelope to Bill.

"Here, you open it." He begins to read out loud:

> We, the judges, have never experienced a performance like you students gave to all of us this morning during the sight-reading competition. We purposely selected a very difficult number for you, believing if you could play sixty percent of the notes correctly and pay attention to fifty percent of the dynamics, it would be an outstanding accomplishment. You proved us wrong. You played *The Hero Overture* close to perfection. We did not think it possible. Indeed, you and your fine director, Jake Dalke, are to be congratulated on winning first in the nation in the category of sight-reading.

Maybe the day Jake laid his baton down and asked everyone to pass in their music was the most significant moment in the life of the band. His telegram simply said:

> MAY 13 MARCHING FIRST, CONCERT FIRST, SIGHT-READING FIRST. HOME TONIGHT BY 9:30.
> JJDALKE

## Shared Healing and Decency

**St. John High School Band Wins National**

Jake's band had been a bridge spanning many troubled waters. Oh, these kids didn't bring wheat out of dry soil, or stop impending wars, or fill the empty pockets of a little town. But they did remind townsfolk that wandering spirits and broken hearts can begin to mend to the beat of a drum and the harmony of a classic overture.

# Epilogue

*Thirty-eight years later*

As St. John prepared for its centennial celebration, the organizing committee studied the past hundred years to determine the most significant events. When they came to the years 1934-1941, there was no question as to who or what had made the most important contribution to the St. John community . . . The St. John Marching and Concert Band.

Dad and Mom sent invitations to all past band members of those special years. Many of the students were not only alive but living in the area. On May 26, 1979, Jake's Band gathered in the St. John community center to renew old friendships and tell the stories of how they won all those national contests. Many of them had not been together since their teenage years. They were casually dressed in canvas shoes to support their marching. It would not seem too different from when they practiced from 7 to 8 a.m. and then hurried to their 8:10 classes, panting and complaining that Mr. Dalke lost track of the time.

They leaned forward then backward in their chairs, surveying faces. Many smiles emerged. With quick steps to connect and embrace one another, they offered polite words that only bordered on the truth. "Oh, my gosh, you haven't changed a bit!"

Arm in arm, thirty-five happy souls roamed about and stared at the many pictures and headlines that had been framed and placed on the walls of this old building. Each picture reminded the

# Epilogue

women and men of a specific time, a trip, a parade and an anxious moment when they waited to hear contest results.

A grown-up John David, the mascot of the band, led the group through a memorial service, reading the names of band members who were no longer living. Following the time of remembrance, Jake offered comments of appreciation for their coming back home to the centennial celebration, saying how wonderful it was to see everyone once again. Then he said,

"The best years of my life were spent with all of you, marching and making music in the St. John Band."

His closing comments stirred many emotions. It was an unexpectedly tender time for all present. The band left the building and lined up on the familiar street, where it stood so many times years ago. The "kids" still knew where to stand. Lisa scrambled to find her place on the pivot. The four ornery sousaphone players held down the back row. Trombones were in front, and Bill stood tall at the front of the band, a large wand held high. Lois had also brought her baton and lined up right behind Bill. Then there was David, with a sign around his neck that said "Mascot." Jake stood beside the band as he always did. They were ready, once again. The professor of music cupped his hands around his wrinkled mouth and shouted boldly, "Band, attention!"

Bill blew his whistle—one long and then four short bursts—that could be heard all over the little town. "Forward, march!"

And, indeed they did, all around the square, with their knees lifted high and their toes pointed.

**The St. John, Kansas Tiger Marching and Concert Band**

J.J. Dalke, Bandmaster, 1934-1941, St. John, Kansas

www.ingramcontent.com/pod-product-compliance
Lightning Source LLC
Chambersburg PA
CBHW070248100426
42743CB00011B/2176